The LORD replied to Moses, "Whoever has sinned against me **I will blot out of my book.**" (Exo 32:33)

They have acted corruptly toward him; to their shame **they are no longer his children**, but a warped and crooked generation. (Deu 32:5)

Those who are far from you will perish; **you destroy all who are unfaithful to you.** (Psa 73:27)

But those who turn to crooked ways the LORD will **banish with the evildoers.** (Psa 125:5)

A man who strays from the path of understanding **comes to rest in the company of the dead.** (Prov 21:16)

. . . those who forsake the LORD **will perish.** (Isa 1:28)

Yet they rebelled and grieved his Holy Spirit. So **he turned and became their enemy** and he himself fought against them. (Isa 63:10)

"Israel was holy to the LORD, the firstfruits of his harvest; all who devoured her were held guilty, and disaster overtook them," declares the LORD. Hear the word of the LORD, O house of Jacob, all you clans of the house of Israel. This is what the LORD says: "What fault did your fathers find in me, that they strayed so far from me? **They followed worthless idols and became worthless themselves.**" (Jer 2:3-5)

Only **hold on to what you have until I come.** (Rev 2:25)

Contents

Introduction

This book is a refutation to eternal security. While our 801 page book, *The Believer's Conditional Security* (TBCS), goes into much more detail, as well as including full documentation on this subject, *The Myth of Eternal Security* will add some additional insights **not found** in the former book, besides reinforcement. This book is also much smaller in size and therefore not so intimidating to book readers.

The best way to depict eternal security is by calling it *the security-in-sin gospel,* for that is exactly what it is. Since the doctrine of eternal security continues to be unashamedly and boldly proclaimed from influential places, Christians who know the truth must likewise be aggressive and fearless in contending for the faith against these *grace changers* (Jude 3,4), who will try to force the Scriptures to allow for every excuse to sin. **Precious souls hang in the balance.**

Make no mistake about it, the believer's endurance is a *salvation* issue and nothing less. It is not merely a *rewards* issue as the eternal security teachers try to reduce it to. This becomes clear as we ponder Scriptures like the following two:

All men will hate you because of me, but he who stands firm to the end **will be saved.** (Mat 10:22)

We have come to share in Christ if we hold firmly till the end the confidence we had at first. (Heb 3:14)

Furthermore, **living godly is not optional for entering God's kingdom** because of *grace,* the infinite work of Christ, the love of God or anything else. However, from the way the *security-in-sin gospel* preachers por-

iii

tray the Christian's liberty and freedoms in Christ, that is not their message. **Though vehemently denied, the** *security-in-sin* **teachers are always trying to make the Christian think he can be ungodly, unholy, evil, worldly, fruitless, unfaithful, immoral, etc. and still remain saved.** This is the bottom line difference between their counterfeit *gospel* and the real gospel found in the Scriptures:

> But now that you have been **set free from sin** and have **become slaves to God,** the benefit you reap leads to **holiness,** and the result is **eternal life.** (Rom 6:22)

> Blessed are the **pure in heart, for they will see God.** (Mat 5:8)

> Make every effort to live in peace with all men and **to be holy**; **without holiness no one will see the Lord.** (Heb 12:14)

Just today as this *Foreword* is being written the following grieving email came to us:

> My husband of 35 years is living in sin with another married woman who is 20 years younger than he is. This is the second time that I know of that he had done this in our marriage. He accepted our Lord and Savior in 1983 after committing adultery with our neighbor and after 5 yrs of marriage counseling on and off I thought our marriage was ok. Now he has been supporting this married woman and living with her for over 10 months now refusing to support me in any way and has filed for divorce last Jan . . . . I told my husband his soul is in jeopardy but **he says his soul is just fine and that any sin he commits is just fine with Jesus because he is saved and any other sin he commits is ok because he is saved!** He continues to live in sin with this woman and is now engaged to marry her as soon as both our divorces go through! I have grieved many months over this and **almost had a breakdown** but have recovered with the Grace of God . . . .

This email came about two weeks later:

My wife of 28 years left me for the man she had had a secret affair with for over 20 years **after they became convinced that they were eternally secure!!** I know this because I recorded their phone calls and she said to him, "Just think we could have been together for 20 years had we known then what we know now," and he said "What's that," and she said "You know . . . . eternal security," and said "Oh yeah, that's right!!" **You are dead on right . . . . the teaching of once saved always saved is demon inspired!! The divorce was devastating to me and my children!!** . . . My ex and her new husband are telling people they are soul mates and were always meant to be together!! **They are even starting a ministry based on these heresies!!** God Bless.

One can only wonder how many **broken homes, drug addictions, suicides, criminal acts, etc.** have occurred because people have been deceived, as the aforementioned adulterers, that their *souls* are just fine in their unrepentant state. **Such people need to know that they must repent (turn from sin) for salvation's sake, which the eternal security teachers could never declare. Hence, there is a tremendous need to combat the diabolical teaching of once saved always saved (OSAS) in any and every way.**

May the Lord God be pleased to use this book to bring many to repentance from their sins and equip Christians with answers about this issue. GOD BLESS YOU.

(Special thanks to Cheryl, my precious wife, for her faithful dedication to the work of God, because without her diligent labors this book you are now reading would not be there!)

Sincerely in Jesus,
Dan Corner

1

The Righteous Can Die Spiritually

There are many death blows to eternal security found in Scripture. At the very core of this doctrine is the concept that a person once saved (a righteous person) will not die spiritually over his sin. The clarity of the Scriptures to the contrary is overwhelming from Genesis through Revelation starting with the first time God ever spoke to Adam, which was his only commandment for him to observe and the consequence of disobedience:

> And the LORD God commanded the man, "You are free to eat from any tree in the garden; but you must not eat from the tree of the knowledge of good and evil, for when you eat of it **you will surely die.**" (Gen 2:16,17)

Adam was *righteous* and resided in the garden of Eden, a paradise garden only for the righteous. He was expelled from it after he sinned and *died*, as warned. **Adam *died* spiritually the same day he sinned**, yet lived physically many years afterwards to be 930 years old (Gen. 5:5). As God's first statement about sin was issued to a righteous man concerning his own spiritual death through sin, the devil's first lie was devised to make Eve dismiss this eternal truth, which led to her disobedience and spiritual death. **Please note that Eve never sinned until she was deceived into thinking that sin would not bring about her own spiritual death. Furthermore, the doctrine of eternal security is *identical* to the devil's first lie, that is, the righteous will not die spiritually through sin:**

"You will not surely die," the serpent said to the woman. (Gen 3:4)

This same consequence of disobedience for the *righteous* is repeated later by the prophet Ezekiel:

Again, when **a righteous man turns from his righteousness and does evil**, and I put a stumbling block before him, **he will die.** Since you did not warn him, he will **die for his sin.** The righteous things he did will not be remembered, and I will hold you accountable for his blood. (Ezek 3:20)

But if a righteous man turns from his righteousness and commits sin and does the same detestable things the wicked man does, will he live? None of the righteous things he has done will be remembered. Because of the unfaithfulness he is guilty of and because of the sins he has committed, **he will die.** (Ezek 18:24)

If a righteous man turns from his righteousness and commits sin, he will die for it; because of the sin he has committed **he will die.** (Ezek 18:26)

If I tell the righteous man that he will surely live, but then he trusts in his righteousness and does evil, none of the righteous things he has done will be remembered; **he will die for the evil he has done.** (Ezek 33:13)

If a righteous man turns from his righteousness and does evil, he will die for it. (Ezek 33:18)

Clearly, a righteous person can die spiritually because of his sin, which again is the antithesis of the teaching of eternal security.

New Testament warnings to the righteous about them dying through sin are repeated, especially by Paul and James. The familiarity between these and the Gen. 2:17 and Ezekiel passages is evident:

For if you live according to the sinful nature, **you will die**; but if by the Spirit you put to death the misdeeds of the body, you will live. (Rom 8:13)

Don't you know that when you offer yourselves to someone to obey him as slaves, you are slaves to the one whom you obey—**whether you are slaves to sin, which leads to death,** or to obedience, which leads to righteousness? (Rom 6:16)

Those Scriptures are written to the *saints* at Rome, who were *righteous*:

To all in Rome who are loved by God and called to be **saints**: Grace and peace to you from God our Father and from the Lord Jesus Christ. First, I thank my God through Jesus Christ for all of you, because **your faith is being reported all over the world.** (Rom. 1:7,8)

By the way, if the reader would compare Rom. 8:13 to Gal. 5:19-21 and 6:8,9, where Paul wrote the same truth three different ways, it becomes unmistakable that he was referring to **the spiritual death of the righteous** (not physical death) for those who live according to the sinful nature because he compared *you will die* in Rom. 8:13 to *not inherit the kingdom of God* in Gal. 5:19-21 and *reap destruction* instead of *reap eternal life* in Gal. 6:8,9. **Apparently Paul repeatedly warned Christians of this possibility, unlike our dark day which denies these same eternal truths. Especially focus on Gal. 5:21.**

James describes the sinning process, which leads to the spiritual death of the righteous:

but each one is tempted when, by his own evil desire, he is dragged away and enticed. **Then, after desire has conceived, it gives birth to sin; and sin, when it is full-grown, gives birth to death.** Don't be deceived, my dear brothers. (James 1:14-16)

As already shown this sinning process to spiritual death dates back to the Garden of Eden, then to Ezekiel, then to Paul the *grace* teacher. James elaborated upon this eternal truth at the very end of his own epistle:

My brethren, if any among you strays from the truth, and one turns him back, let him know that he who turns a sinner from the error of his way **will save his soul from death**, and will cover over a multitude of sins. (James 5:19,20, NASB)

Notice how straying from the *truth* (a name for Jesus in John 14:6) is to jeopardize the soul of the righteous person to (eternal) *death*. But if that same person is brought back where he was before he strayed, his *soul* will once again be safe (or saved) in *the truth*. Also shown here is the fact that **a saved person can become a *sinner* again, by straying from the truth.**

How the *Righteous* Can Prevent Their Own Spiritual Death

The Lord Himself taught how the righteous can prevent their own spiritual death:

I tell you the truth, if anyone keeps my word, **he will never see death.** (John 8:51)

Clearly, the Lord was not talking about physical death, since many righteous people remained faithful to the very end, such as the Apostle Paul did, yet died physically. Again, since Paul died physically, Jesus couldn't have been referring to physical death. Hence, the Lord gave the preventative to spiritual death as being simply to *keep* his word or **continue to obey** to the end.

Jesus restated the same eternal *safeguard* for spiritual death in different words when he spoke the following:

Jesus said to her, "I am the resurrection and the life. He who believes in me will live, even though he dies; and whoever lives and believes in me will never die. **Do you believe this?"** (John 11:25,26)

The word translated "believes" in v. 26 is a *continuous* tense in the Greek. Jesus declared that the righteous would *never die* spiritually as long as they maintained this type of belief, which is shown elsewhere as being a trusting, submitting, obeying faith which produces good fruit and holy behavior. **In other words, the Lord was saying in John 11 that** a righteous person would have to continue to believe so he would not die spiritually, which does not always happen. **The Lord taught elsewhere that it is possible for a believer to become an unbeliever, at which point he would *fall away* as a result:**

> Those on the rock are the ones who **receive the word** with joy when they hear it, but they have no root. **They believe for a while**, but in the time of testing they **fall away.** (Luke 8:13)

That was the Lord's own interpretation of the following verse:

> Some fell on rock, and when it came up, the plants **withered** because they had no moisture. (Luke 8:6)

To save their doctrine, the eternal security teachers (the Scripture distorters) sometimes amazingly argue that the people of Luke 8:13 only had a *spurious* or *false* faith, but that is not the text speaking—just their own faulty theology. Not only does Lk. 8:13 say such people did *believe for a while*, it also states that they *receive the word with joy*. Real, genuine plant *life*, likened unto spiritual life, sprung up from the word of God, which was *received* with joy. The problem is such don't continue with God because they fail the test of persecution for godly living.

They *Received the Word*

To *receive the word* as in Luke 8:13 is the same description of what happened to Cornelius and his household who **experienced true salvation.** Just before Peter retold what happened with them we read:

> The apostles and the brothers throughout Judea heard that the Gentiles also had *received the word of God.* (Acts 11:1)

Similar to that are two additional Scriptures which refer to others who likewise *received the word* of God. According to the context, such describes that they got saved after receiving the word of God:

> But when they believed Philip preaching the things concerning the kingdom of God, and the name of Jesus Christ, they were baptized, both men and women. Then Simon himself believed also: and when he was baptized, he continued with Philip, and wondered, beholding the miracles and signs which were done. Now when the apostles which were at Jerusalem heard that Samaria had **received the word of God**, they sent unto them Peter and John: (Acts 8:12-14, KJV)

These were more noble than those in Thessalonica, in that they **received the word** with all readiness of mind, and searched the scriptures daily, whether those things were so. **Therefore many of them believed**; also of honourable women which were Greeks, and of men, not a few. (Acts 17:11,12, KJV)

Please note that the same Greek work translated *received* in Luke 8:13 is also found in Acts 8:14; 11:1 and 17:11. Luke 8:13 is referring to people who had experienced true salvation, just like these other Scriptures do because such people *received* the word. Yet the Luke 8:13 passage states **they ceased believing.**

Getting back to John 8:51 and 11:25,26, the Lord shared the same facts as stated there in yet a different Scripture, also from John:

I tell you the truth, **he who believes has everlasting life.** I am the bread of life. Your forefathers ate the manna in the desert, yet they died. But here is the bread that comes down from heaven, which a **man may eat and not die.** I am the living bread that came down from heaven. **If anyone eats of this bread, he will live forever.** This bread is my flesh, which I will give for the life of the world. (John 6:47-51)

Please note the word *believes* in v. 47 is also a *continuous* tense in the Greek. Believing in Jesus is compared to eating the *bread of life,* which will prevent spiritual death, and enable one to *live forever.* **We eat this** *bread* **by continuing or maintaining our submissive faith in Jesus, that same truth as shown at John 11:25,26.** When one continues to believe he will *keep* God's word, the preventative for the righteous dying spiritually, as stated in John 8:51.

At another time, the Lord spoke to those on the very edge of spiritual death in Rev. 3:2:

Wake up! Strengthen what remains **and is about to die**, for I have not found your deeds complete in the sight of my God.

Please note it was the personal responsibility of the ones *about to die* to *strengthen* themselves spiritually. God was not going to do it for them, even though it was His will for them to be strengthened. The spiritual negligence and sloth of the righteous can be fatal.

Be Faithful, Even to the Point of Death

The Rev. 3:2 passage is similar to the warning given by the Lord in the preceding chapter to faithful Christians:

> Do not be afraid of what you are about to suffer. I tell you, the devil will put some of you in prison to test you, and you will suffer persecution for ten days. **Be faithful, even to the point of death**, and I will give you the crown of life. He who has an ear, let him hear what the Spirit says to the churches. **He who overcomes will not be hurt at all by the second death.** (Rev 2:10,11)

Certainly, spiritual death is implied since the faithful Christians at Smyrna were warned by Jesus to continue being faithful to the point of physical death (to *overcome*), so that they would not be *hurt at all by the second death.* The second death is another name for *the lake of fire* (Rev. 20:14; 21:8).

So what happens to a person with spiritual life (a Christian) who is not faithful to the end of his life? He will die spiritually. This possibility of the righteous dying spiritually is reiterated yet another time by the Lord himself, yet ends joyfully because he repents and returns to salvation:

> For this son of mine **was dead and is alive again**; he **was lost** and is found. So they began to celebrate. (Luke 15:24)

> But we had to celebrate and be glad, because this brother of yours **was dead and is alive again**; he **was lost** and is found. (Luke 15:32)

Please note that the prodigal was spiritually *dead* and spiritually *lost* at the same point in time, that is when he was in sexual immorality and wild living. After he repented he became *alive again.* Those words are very important. It says *again.* That means he had spiritual life before he left the Father to indulge in wild living and sexual immorality. He got that same spiritual life back again when he repented and returned to serve the Father. In other words, he was righteous yet died spiritually through sin (became *lost*) and later became spiritually alive *again* when he turned from his wickedness to serve God. (This is Jesus' teaching not some cultist or so-called *works salvation* person.) Hence, as Jesus taught elsewhere that one passes from spiritual death to spiritual life at the point of getting born again, He also taught the same person can pass back from spiritual life to spiritual death through sin, as happened to the prodigal.

This same truth about spiritual death for the righteous is echoed by the Apostle John in his first epistle:

> If anyone sees his brother commit a sin that does not lead to death, he should pray and God will give him life. I refer to those whose sin does not lead to death. **There is a sin that leads to death**. I am not saying that he should pray about that. (1 John 5:16)

John wrote about the spiritual death of the righteous here. He stated that sin would bring that about as happened to Adam, as well as the prodigal. Another definite example of a righteous man dying, but not physically, was King David when he turned to do evil. Ezekiel warned such a righteous person *will die*, yet **David continued to live physically as did Adam and the prodigal.** These facts, of course, are all opposed by the eternal security teachers who want us to believe the devil's teaching, as stated in Gen. 3:4. They agree with the devil and try to confuse the issue by saying the *death* of 1 John 5:16 is physical death, with Ananias and Sapphira being examples. In other words, they believe God in his wrath over their sin of lying to the Holy Spirit struck them dead in their unrepentant wickedness and rewarded them by taking them quicker into His paradise kingdom, which is reserved only for the *holy* and *pure of heart.* By teaching like this the eternal security teachers not only proclaim a license for immorality, but also contradict yet another Scripture, which shows that *all liars* will go to *the lake of fire*:

> But the cowardly, the unbelieving, the vile, the murderers, the sexually immoral, those who practice magic arts, the idolaters and **all liars** —their place will be in the **fiery lake of burning sulfur**. This is the second death. (Rev 21:8)

For some reason the eternal security teachers seem oblivious to Scriptures which show that God does sometimes strike the *wicked* (or unsaved) physically dead for their sin:

> But Er, Judah's firstborn, **was wicked** in the Lord's sight; so **the LORD put him to death**. (Gen 38:7)

Those Widows *Died* Spiritually

Last but not least, let's not forget the widows of 1 Tim. 5:6, about whom Paul wrote:

But the widow who lives for pleasure **is dead even while she lives**.

Immediately afterwards, he refers to some widows that turned from their *dedication* to Christ (v. 11) to *follow Satan* (v. 15). Notice: those widows Paul knew didn't die physically, yet were *dead* (spiritually) because of their sins. This passage doesn't refer to those never saved, as we may assume could be the case in Lk. 9:60 and Mt. 8:22, but instead to those who were once alive spiritually like the prodigal, because they previously had a *dedication* to Christ and later turned away from it.

Green renders 1 Tim. 5:6, as follows:

But she who lives in self-pleasure **has died** *while* living.

Dear reader, don't be deceived by those parroting the devil's first lie to our generation, the eternal security teachers. The Bible is clear that the righteous will *die* spiritually, if they turn to do evil, as Adam, King David, the prodigal, the widows of 1 Tim. 5:6, etc. did. If you are a real Christian, you must faithfully follow Jesus and endure persecution for living godly to the end of your life to enter God's kingdom. Don't be deceived by the false teachers who want to convince you otherwise. Much more information regarding the subject of eternal security is found in our 801 page book, *The Believer's Conditional Security*, which is the most exhaustive and comprehensive refutation to this false doctrine ever written.

2 ─────────────────────────

Pairs Of Truths

How is it possible for false doctrine to run rampant in a day with so many Bibles within easy reach? **In part, it is because false teachers are convincingly presenting a partial truth as the whole truth and distorting its intended meaning. This has often been done by the eternal security teachers, who flood TV, radio and literature with their counterfeit version of grace and the gospel.**

The following list of supplementary truths will help the Christian combat this sinister message of our day that is openly proclaimed and widely received. The grace changers and their sin-gospel have done incalculable harm, as grace is turned into a license to sin by declaring that sin will not keep a Christian out of the kingdom of heaven.

This chapter should help with this deception. The first half of the following statements are readily known, while the second half are hardly recognized by many as being found in the Scriptures!

Please freely copy this important list and spread it to all of your Christian friends and family.

- We are saved by grace (Eph. 2:8,9), **but we can fall from grace (Gal. 5:2-4).**
- We are justified by faith (Rom. 5:1), **but our faith can cease to exist (Luke 8:13; Rom. 11:19-23) and become shipwrecked (1 Tim. 1:19,20).**
- We are not under the law (Rom. 6:14,15), **but if you live according to the sinful nature you will die (Rom. 8:13).**

■ Paul taught against legalism (Gal. 5:3,4), but among others things he taught:

But among you there **must not be even a hint of sexual immorality, or of any kind of impurity, or of greed,** because these are improper for God's holy people. Nor should there be **obscenity, foolish talk or coarse joking,** which are out of place, but rather thanksgiving. For of this you can be sure: **No immoral, impure or greedy person— such a man is an idolater—has any inheritance in the kingdom of Christ and of God. Let no one deceive you with empty words,** for because of such things God's wrath comes on those who are disobedient. Therefore do not be partners with them (Eph. 5:3-6).

■ We are not saved by works (Eph. 2:8,9), **but to reap eternal life and not destruction, you must sow to please the Spirit and not the sinful nature (Gal. 6:8,9).**
■ God is faithful to us (1 John 1:9; 1 Cor. 10:13), **but we must be faithful to him to the very end of our lives to escape the lake of fire, or second death (Rev. 2:10,11).**
■ God surely loves us (John 3:16; Mk. 10:21; Rom. 8:35-39), **but those who inherit the kingdom of God love God (James 2:5 cf. 1 Cor. 2:9). And to love God means to *obey* his commandments (Jn. 14:15; 1 John 5:3).**
■ We have freedom in Christ (Gal. 5:1), **but this freedom is not to indulge the sinful nature (Gal. 5:13; 1 Pet. 2:16).**

To be sound, a teaching must be Biblical. To stress only a partial truth, with a distorted interpretation, as eternal security teachers do, is to mislead multitudes down the primrose path to destruction.

Summary

In summary, never forget:

■ The Bible is final authority for the Christian (2 Tim. 3:16,17).
■ The whole message needs to sought out on any given topic, including the believer's security.
■ The aforementioned eternal truths are not heresy, legalism, works, etc., as some will falsely accuse. If they are, then the Lord and His

apostles were also guilty of the same, for these truths originated with them.

■ False teachers will be here to the very end deceiving many (2 Pet. 2:1,2).

■ **To enter the kingdom of God Christians must endure hatred and persecution to the very end of their lives (Mt. 10:22; Heb. 3:14; Rev. 2:10,11); live holy (Rom. 6:22; Heb. 12:14); bring forth good fruit (Mt. 7:19); and do good (John 5:29), according to New Testament grace.**

3

Eternal Security: Could It Be A Doctrine Of Demons?

It's an awesome thought to consider the capabilities of demons! Among other things, demons actually formulate teachings (1 Tim. 4:1)! Since Satan can readily quote Scripture (Mt. 4:6), we should not think the teachings of demons will be filled with apparent gaping holes that can be easily noticed with little or no effort.

Also, the way Satan succeeded in verbally communicating his wishes for Job to "curse God" (Job 1:11; 2:5) through his wife (2:9) is astounding! But it is even more astounding that Satan actually spoke through Peter, one of the Lord's chosen apostles (Mt. 16:22,23)!

Should we, then, consider it ludicrous for a "doctrine of demons" to come through respected and popular teachers of our day? Most assuredly not!

There is one thing we can be sure of. The devil **only** has our eternal harm in mind! In other words, he will try to harm us, especially spiritually. One of the best ways to do this is to downplay the ultimate danger of sin, while not going too far in the other direction so as to be easily detected. This is exactly what the teaching of eternal security does! By this I mean, eternal security teachers will readily preach against sin—openly declaring the pain, shame and regret it brings, even the loss of eternal rewards and one's position in the kingdom, but will never declare such has the potential of keeping a person who was once saved out of the kingdom all together, in spite of the many clear Scriptures which show this possibility (Rom. 8:13; Gal. 5:19-21; 6:8; Rev. 22:19; etc.)! Seemingly, this fact has been hidden from their Biblical understanding for some reason. We should not be surprised that large numbers of people will be attracted to this type of message! See 2 Tim. 4:3,4.

Does True Grace Teaching Allow The Sexually Immoral In Heaven?

With all this in mind, we need to ask a revealing and vital question: Does true grace teaching allow the sexually immoral in heaven? Why have I singled out the sin of sexual immorality? Because this is obviously a sex-crazed society in which we live. In general, Jesus called it an "adulterous" generation (Mk. 8:38). Moreover, Paul said we would have to escape the planet to get away from, among others, the sexually immoral (1 Cor. 5:10)!

But what does the Bible say about the **seriousness** of sexual sin? This is where something begins to surface that is not very pleasant! By this I mean the devil and his "doctrine of demons." For centuries those who teach the myth of eternal security have denied and vehemently argued against sexual immorality negating one's salvation. Sometimes the patriarch David is mentioned in such an endeavor, as done by the deceased John R. Rice:

> David committed sins of murder and adultery. We must condemn his sins. They were bad. But David's sins were under the blood of Christ, and in the fifty-first Psalm, the prayer of David shows that he had not lost his salvation, but the joy of salvation.

By quoting a reference, John R. Rice seemingly backs his beloved position with the authoritative Scriptures. However, if one would check Psalm 51, he would see that Rice has "read into" the Scriptures something that is not there as the basis for his argument! Please note: **Nowhere in Psalm 51 does it say that David did not lose his salvation!** We only read here of his prayerful wishes to have the joy of his salvation restored! But was the loss of the joy of his salvation the extreme limit of the spiritual harm he did to himself by his single act of sexual immorality (and murder)? Let's allow the Apostle Paul to answer this for us. In 1 Cor. 6:9,10, Paul (in question form) clears this issue up once and for all:

> Do you not know that the wicked will not inherit the kingdom of God? Do not be deceived: Neither the **sexually immoral** nor idolaters nor **adulterers** nor **male prostitutes** nor **homosexuals** nor

thieves nor the greedy nor drunkards nor slanderers nor swindlers will inherit the kingdom of God.

This is what the great grace teacher openly taught as part of his gospel message. Wow! Doesn't that help identify those "doctrines of demons" we need to be aware of? **Real *grace* teaching declares that all unforgiven sexually immoral people, besides others like drunkards and the greedy, will definitely not enter the kingdom of God. There are no exceptions!**
To reiterate, the eternal security teachers are openly contradicting Paul's grace message about the sexually immoral entering heaven! (Of course, they are very careful to stay away from 1 Cor. 6:9,10 as they teach bits and pieces of the Bible, focusing in upon and emphasizing certain verses which, on the surface, seem to be backing for their doctrine.)
Another very clear refutation to eternal security, also written by Paul, is the following:

> **For of this you can be sure**: No immoral, impure or greedy person— such a man is an idolater—has any inheritance in the kingdom of Christ and of God. **Let no one deceive you with empty words**, for because of such things God's wrath comes on those who are disobedient. Therefore, do not be partners with them. (Eph. 5:5-7)

This was Paul's "assurance message" in his day. Friends, the Bible says, "let no one deceive you with empty words" about the immoral, impure or greedy, that is, even if they come from a person on TV, radio and who has written numerous books, some of which, overall, are very sound in doctrine!
I wish I could say this type of spiritual poison about sexual sin has only been taught in the past by John R. Rice. However, this is certainly not the case.
Even more blatant in his teaching on eternal security, Bob George declared his distorted interpretation of one of Paul's teachings over dozens of radio stations:

> And as Paul said, "All things are permissible, but not all things are profitable." **So is committing fornication permissible**? YES. Is it profitable? No, it isn't.

Perhaps Bob George should read 1 Cor. 6:9,10 and Eph. 5:5-7, among other clear verses. Furthermore, all advocates of this type of teaching should focus in upon Titus 2:12 which describes the true grace of God:

It teaches us to say **"No" to ungodliness and worldly passions, and to live self-controlled, upright and godly lives in this present age.**

Imagine the incredible influence that other eternal security teachers like Charles Stanley and John MacArthur have in our country at this time. These men are pastors of congregations in excess of 10,000 each! Furthermore, their radio broadcasts are heard everywhere in the United States with almost no exception. Television is also a channel through which their easy-to-receive message regarding eternal security is broadcasted alongside their sound sermons. Moreover, Stanley was elected president at least twice of the convention held by the largest Protestant denomination in the United States, that is, the Southern Baptist. Truly, his influence alone is phenomenal. Yet these ministries, along with Bob George and many others, are openly and shockingly teaching our generation that true grace teaching does allow the sexually immoral in heaven!

Let's give God Himself (seated on His throne) the final word about the sexually immoral:

But the cowardly, the unbelieving, the vile, the murderers, **the sexually immoral**, those who practice magic arts, the idolaters and all liars—**their place will be in the fiery lake of burning sulfur.** This is the second death. (Rev. 21:8)

Could anything be more clear than this?

Eternal Security Is Spiritually Dangerous

In light of all of this, without equivocation, I believe **it is spiritually dangerous for the Body of Christ to be exposed to the teaching of eternal security!** This is the only logical conclusion one can come to since the Bible clearly identifies this type of sinner (the sexually immoral) as **hell bound** and not just something less, as the eternal security teachers are saying. In other words, **the seriousness of sexual immorality, as taught by the eternal security teachers, is as far from the truth of God as the lake**

of fire is from the kingdom of God! Should not this teaching, therefore, be exposed and refuted? Obviously, I believe it's crucial to do so.

Regarding this rampant teaching, my wife and I were recently listening to a tape on a subject that we thought would have nothing to do with endorsing eternal security. We were wrong! The teacher was doing fine until he subtly slipped in the doctrine of eternal security:

> ... But he would use them [girls], and he used them sexually at times as well. Now **this is a guy in the Body of Christ.**[1]

Gunderson should have said, "Now this guy was a professing Christian, but by his actions he denied the Lord (Titus 1:16)" or "He fell into sexual sin as the Prodigal did (Lk. 15:30) and therefore was in vital need of repentance for salvation's sake (Lk. 15:24)."

Those of us who know of the spiritual danger of eternal security should be openly speaking out against this pernicious doctrine, which has to be adversely affecting multitudes in our day. It is time for true servants of God to clearly and boldly proclaim the truth of God! Souls hang in the balance. Many will be misled to Hell through eternal security, unless there are clear voices openly refuting it. What will **you** do to help remedy this horrible situation? Remember this: The eternal security teachers, with their incredible influence, won't hesitate to continue to openly pour out their spiritually dangerous "myths" over radio, tv and in their literature!

For just one reason why this is so, consider what Charles Stanley wrote:

> The very gospel itself comes under attack when the **eternal security of the believer is questioned.**[2]

What an unbelievable statement! Yet, sadly, many believe it. God only knows how many people in **your** circle of influence are of this number and could be spiritually hurt by this type of bold assertion unless **you** do something! The time to act is now.

---

1   The Theater Of Your Mind—What's Showing? (Tape 2) by Denny Gunderson.
2   *Eternal Security: Can You Be Sure?* (Thomas Nelson Publishers, 1990), p.192, emphasis ours.

I, personally, will openly stand against the rampant false doctrine of eternal security, just like I will stand against any other dangerous distortion of the gospel of grace in an effort to please my Lord!

In conclusion then, does **true grace teaching** allow the sexually immoral in heaven? One group would answer "No," the other "Yes." One group is right, the other wrong. One is God's truth, the other is the devil's lie!

4

Did Jesus Teach Eternal Security?

Though there are many teachings of the Lord Jesus that we could focus in upon to answer this question, perhaps His teaching known as The Prodigal Son (Luke 15:11-32) would be the best of all regarding this controversy. This teaching demonstratively shows the full extent of sin's destructive power in the life of a son of God, the key roles that free will and human responsibility have, the limited protective power offered by the believer's "seal," as taught by Christ Himself and much more. Let's examine it closely.

The teaching starts by focusing in on the younger of the two sons of the father, who asked for and received his share of the estate. Soon afterward, he departed from the father's presence for a distant country of "wild living" (v. 13). There he squandered his wealth with prostitutes (v. 30). After he spent everything he had there was a severe famine in that country, during which time he personally longed to eat the pods that the pigs were eating, but no one gave him anything! He then came to his senses, returned to the father repentfully and found complete forgiveness and restoration. Beyond this, the father with no hesitation initiated the "kill the fattened calf" celebration for his homecoming.

Verses 24 and 32 are essential to this parable, controversy and study. Both of these Scriptures, declared by the father, reveal the spiritual condition of the prodigal both **before** and **after** the time of his "wild living." Verse 24 spoken to his servants says, "For this son of mine **was dead and is alive again; he was lost and is found**," while verse 32, spoken to the older son says, "... this brother of yours **was dead and is alive again; he was lost and is found**." The important point the father was emphasizing

24

was the complete reversal of the prodigal's spiritual condition, now that he repented. He went from "dead" to "alive *again*" **which is equated in the same sentence as going from "lost" to "found.**" Hence, there is great reason to rejoice over such a sinner that repents, as already mentioned two separate times in this same chapter in the parables of the Lost Sheep and Lost Coin.

Perhaps the words "alive *again*" are most revealing. The Greek word from which "alive *again*" comes is found five times in the New Testament—in these two verses just cited, Rom. 7:9; 14:9 and Rev. 20:5. It means live again or revive. This is easily seen in Rom. 14:9, ". . . Christ died and **returned to life . . .**" Here it is stated that the Lord's physical condition went from life <u>to</u> death [on the cross] <u>to</u> **life again** [when He arose from the grave]. Similarly, the prodigal's spiritual condition went from life <u>to</u> death [when with the prostitutes] <u>to</u> life **again** [when he turned from sin and returned to the father's presence]. Regarding this type of action and the believer's security, one strain of eternal security is perhaps best exemplified by what John MacArthur wrote:

> No matter how convincing a person's testimony might seem, once he becomes apostate he has demonstrated irrefutably that he was never really saved.[1]

The Lord Jesus, in contrast to MacArthur, clearly taught by this parable that a person once saved can become lost again! Also see the chapter entitled, *"Never Really Saved"* for other arguments.

Furthermore, there are many in our hour that unfortunately teach and sincerely believe that the most one could ever lose through sin after initial salvation is their joy of salvation, spiritual rewards and/or position in the kingdom. Jesus, however, very clearly taught otherwise! The Lord taught the prodigal's spiritual condition degenerated to "dead," the same as for everyone before initial salvation (Eph. 2:1). Paul stated likewise, after initial salvation, "If you live according to the sinful nature **you will die**, but if by the Spirit you put to death the misdeeds of the body you will live" (Rom. 8:13). **This is what happened to the prodigal, that is, he died**

---

1   John F. MacArthur, Jr., *The Gospel According to Jesus* (Zondervan Publishing, Grand Rapids, MI, 1989), p. 98.

spiritually because he chose, through his own free will, to "live according to the sinful nature."

Luke 15:13 states "wild living" characterized his behavior when spiritually "dead" and "lost" in his unconfessed and unrepented sins. The word for "wild living" comes from the Greek word meaning excess, as found in Eph. 5:18: "And be not drunk with wine, wherein is **excess**; but be filled with the Spirit" (KJV). Hence, the prodigal's behavior, as implied by Lk. 15:13, could have included drunkenness and other excesses that go with that kind of sinful lifestyle. This would be a safe assumption anyway, especially since he spent his money with prostitutes! If so, among other grievous sins, the prodigal's sins were sexual immorality and drunkenness —two rampant spiritual killers in our day too! Paul wrote about these and other similar sins in Gal. 5:19-21 and 1 Cor. 6:9,10. This former passage, written to Christians in warning form, reads:

> The acts of the sinful nature are obvious: **sexual immorality**, impurity and debauchery; idolatry and witchcraft; hatred, discord, jealousy, fits of rage, selfish ambition, dissensions, factions and envy; **drunkenness**, orgies, and the like. **I warn you, as I did before, that those who live like this will not inherit the kingdom of God.**

Robert B. Thieme, another influential eternal security teacher of our day, likens the prodigal son to a *carnal Christian* whom he describes as follows:

> The behavior pattern of a carnal Christian cannot be distinguished from that of an unbeliever (1 Cor. 3:3). As far as God's Word is concerned, you may act like an unbeliever; but if you have believed in Christ, you are still a believer—a believer in status quo carnality— out of fellowship. This principle is important in understanding the prodigal. A BELIEVER OUT OF FELLOWSHIP ACTS LIKE AN UNBELIEVER.[2]

What a venomous lie this is! Please know the following about *carnal Christians* as mentioned by Paul:

---

2   R. B. Thieme, Jr., *The Prodigal Son* (Houston, TX, 1974), p. 7. Emphasis his.

■ 1 Cor. 3:3 is very clear about their sins being "jealousy" and "quarreling" and nothing as severe as the Prodigal's were. Paul wrote:

You are still worldly. For since there is jealousy and quarreling among you, are you not worldly? Are you not acting like mere men?

Furthermore, in the next two verses we see why they were acting like this, that is, **some at Corinth apparently favored one Christian leader over another, namely Paul over Apollos and vice versa!**

■ In 1 Cor. 6:11, we read:

And that is what some of you **were**. But you **were** washed, you **were** sanctified, you **were** justified in the name of the Lord Jesus Christ and by the Spirit of our God.

Please note: those "carnal" Christians were not drunkards anymore or sexually immoral anymore, etc., as clearly indicated by the word *were* in this verse referring back to verses 9 and 10! **This again shows an all-important difference between what the eternal security teachers are saying and what God says, as recorded in the Bible.**

■ To believe the eternal security teachers regarding carnal Christianity and the behavior of such people would also render meaningless verses such as 1 Jn. 3:10:

This is how we know who the children of God are and who the children of the devil are: Anyone who does not do what is right is not a child of God; nor is anyone who does not love his brother.

Please note that John's test to know a child of God from a child of the devil was *a present-tense behavioral* one and not just a testimony of a past conversion experience! See also 1 Jn. 2:3,4.
It is my contention that as water is to fire, so the teaching of eternal security is to the fear of God, as evident by eternal security teachings such as these.
Please note: unlike what some of the eternal security teachers would say, based on a faulty interpretation of Col. 2:13, the prodigal's future sins were not automatically forgiven, because if they were, it would have been

impossible for them to bring about his "dead" and "lost" spiritual condition! "He forgave us all our sins" (Col. 2:13), can only refer to "all" of our **past** sins getting forgiven at the point of initial salvation. If not, there would be no need to confess sins committed after salvation for forgiveness, as shown in 1 Jn. 1:9. In addition, many other Scriptures would be meaningless if all our future sins were automatically forgiven also at the point of initial salvation! In contrast to Scripture and reason, another eternal security teacher (June Hunt) said,

> June: "Well, technically, Carl, a person who has truly entered into a relationship with the Lord Jesus Christ, let me ask you this, how many of their sins were forgiven once they entered into that relationship with Him?"
> Carl: "Well, I believe all of mine have been."
> June: "Yes, because that's what Scripture teaches."
> Carl: "Past, present and **future**."
> June: "And **future**. So the issue is, **all of our sins are already forgiven**."[3]

While some heavily rely upon Jesus' promise stated in Jn. 10:28,29, that is, that no one will *snatch* his sheep from His hand or the Father's hand, please note that this doesn't exclude the apparent possibility of a *sheep* walking off due to his own personal free will to a lifestyle that will result in spiritual death, as exemplified by the prodigal son! No one plucked the prodigal out of the Father's hand, but the Father let him walk away! **Also, the wonderful promise of John 10:28,29 holds true only for those who *follow* [continuous tense in the Greek] Jesus (v. 27)!**

Also, many read into the believer's *seal*, which Paul wrote of, as a spiritual protection that is an assurance that will, most definitely, mean our future entrance into the kingdom no matter what. However, Jesus' teaching on the prodigal son also refutes this faulty interpretation, for that *seal* didn't prevent the prodigal's *dead* and *lost* condition from coming about! The same can be emphatically stated from James 4:4b regarding anyone who would *choose to be a friend of the world* and consequently become an *enemy of God*. Enemies of God will be **consumed by raging fire (Heb. 10:27)**! This too shows the *seal* won't prevent their spiritual death.

---

3   June Hunt, tape: *Suicide or Survival,* #9114. Emphasis ours.

Furthermore, in light of Heb. 13:5 which states that God will never leave or forsake us, please note the prodigal left and forsook the father and the father let him walk off! Besides, Heb. 13:5,8 is a quote from Deut. 31:6,8, which shows by Deut. 31:17 that God will *forsake* us because of sin!

Many eternal security proponents try to weaken such truths as these and others taught in the parables by saying things like: Parables weren't given for doctrine or parables teach only one truth and not several! Regarding the latter, Charles Stanley wrote in his monthly magazine:

> Jesus told the story of the prodigal son for one reason, to portray God's unconditional love. (Luke 15:11-32).[4]

Both of these objections are categorically false! **Parables were taught by Christ as a means of revealing the secrets of the kingdom to believers and concealing the same secrets from the unbelievers (Matt. 13:10-13).** Since doctrine is one and the same as teachings, obviously parables are for doctrine. For example, the parable of the Pharisee and Tax Collector (Lk. 18:9-14) clearly teaches the doctrine of instant justification for all, who like that tax collector, sincerely and humbly pray directly to God asking for forgiveness. Furthermore, a second basic truth is clearly taught in the same parable—namely, one must first be aware of his own personal need of forgiveness before he will receive it. The self-righteous pharisee lacked this insight and went home unjustified and unforgiven! Hence, both objections raised by eternal security proponents, against the use of parables, are clearly refuted here!

Finally regarding the prodigal son, let us all rejoice that the father quickly and joyfully took him back after he repented. In other words, we know from this that **a person can get saved more than once based on this teaching and a corroborating one by Paul, the true grace teacher, in Rom. 11:19-23**:

> You will say then, "Branches were broken off so that I could be grafted in." Granted. But they were broken off because of unbelief, and you stand by faith. **Do not be arrogant, but be afraid.** For if God did not spare the natural branches, **he will not spare you either.**

---

4   *In Touch,* September 1994, p. 7.

Consider therefore the kindness and sternness of God: sternness to those who fell, but kindness to you, **provided that you continue in his kindness. Otherwise, you also will be cut off.** And **if they do not persist in unbelief**, they will be grafted in, for **God is able to graft them in** *again.*[5]

Other passages given by Jesus which refute eternal security are: Matt. 6:14,15; 10:22,33; 24:13; 25:26-30; Lk. 8:13; 12:45,46; Jn. 15:6; Rev. 2:10,11,26; 3:15,16.

Come on home modern-day prodigals. God will likewise accept and rejoice over you! Don't think you have sinned too much to return. The prodigal whom Jesus taught about, likewise, knew only *wild living* for an undesignated period of time—perhaps many years. God wants you home in his presence, too—*alive again* and no longer *lost.* Come while you still can.

---

5   This passage from Rom. 11 seems to be tailor-made and customized for this controversy over the believer's security. Clearly, it causes much trouble for the eternal security proponent, that is, if he even knows it exists!

5

Eight Stirring Passages From 1 Timothy

1 Timothy is known as a *pastoral epistle*. All throughout this epistle, Paul gave Timothy instructions to pass on to other Christians regarding how to pray, how women are to dress, how to pick deacons, how to view riches, among other values and church concerns. **Besides all of that, this epistle (just like the Book of Hebrews) especially reveals that there is no such thing as the doctrine is called in our day** *eternal security.* (There are very few, if any, arguments for eternal security that come from 1 Timothy. The eternal security teachers remain silent about this Pauline epistle and even seem to avoid it, when dealing with Paul's *grace* message about the believer's security.)

Let's take a closer look at eight passages regarding the Christian battle and salvation that were basic in the days of first-century Christianity:

> As I urged you when I went into Macedonia, stay there in Ephesus so that you may **command certain men not to teach false doctrines any longer nor to devote themselves to myths and endless genealogies.** These promote controversies rather than God's work—which is by faith. **The goal of this command is love,** which comes from **a pure heart and a good conscience and a sincere faith**. Some have **wandered away from these** and turned to meaningless talk. (1 Tim 1:3-6).

Paul had Timothy stay in Ephesus for an express purpose—to *command certain men not to teach false doctrines any longer nor to devote themselves to myths and endless genealogies.* After he stated this, he then revealed something about himself and the goal of that charge to Timothy which was *love* and that came from Paul's *pure heart and a good conscience and a sincere faith.* **(This is Paul's autobiographical sketch of himself and the exact opposite to the typical way the once saved always saved [OSAS] teachers like to portray him. Paul was a *holy* man, who taught holy living. See also 1 Thess. 2:10.)**

After all of that, Paul sadly refers to *some,* whom he knew, that *wandered away* from the same kind of *pure heart and a good conscience and a sincere faith* that he had, which testifies beyond all doubt to the fact that they were previously saved. See Acts 15:9; Heb. 9:9 and 10:22. Clearly, those men were no longer saved as is evident by their changed *heart, conscience* and *faith.* **In other words, they lost their salvation, even though they had been previously *sealed* by the Holy Spirit, received the *gift* of eternal life and had been saved by *grace.***

That kind of teaching was original Christianity, but is essentially lost or denied in our dark day by wolves standing behind the pulpits.

Hymenaeus and Alexander

A second passage to note is the following one:

Timothy, my son, I give you this instruction in keeping with the prophecies once made about you, so that by following them you may fight the good fight, **holding on to faith and a good conscience. Some have rejected these and so have shipwrecked their faith. Among them are Hymenaeus and Alexander**, whom I have handed over to Satan to be taught not to blaspheme. (1 Tim 1:18-20)

Paul again mentions *faith* and a *good conscience.* He told Timothy that it was his own personal responsibility to *hold* on to these for his own salvation's sake—so his saving faith wouldn't become *shipwrecked.* (God wasn't going to *hold* on to these for him.) Paul added because Hymenaeus and Alexander didn't do this very thing, their faith did become *shipwrecked* and they were now blaspheming! **Paul knew that same horrible end could occur to Timothy (or any Christian person in our modern day) and gave the cited safeguards to prevent such, which were all under the original *grace* message.** In other words, Hymenaeus and Alexander both had (past tense) what Timothy had (present tense) at that moment as a Christian, but **Paul knew Timothy could lose it.**

Timothy apparently acted on these vital safeguards, as Paul taught him here, for later Paul mentions Timothy's *sincere faith*, which he was apparently still *holding* on to:

I have been reminded of your **sincere faith**, which first lived in your grandmother Lois and in your mother Eunice and, I am persuaded, **now lives in you also.** (2 Tim 1:5)

The Warning About Picking Overseers

Passage three is the following one:

He must not be a recent convert, or **he may become conceited and fall under the same judgment as the devil.** (1 Tim 3:6)

The context of verse 6 starts at chapter 3, verse 1. The subject is the spiritual qualifications for *overseers* in a local assembly. **Paul states his godly concerns that a spiritual fatality, through *pride*, could occur if a new Christian is given such a high position.** (Sometimes the most zealous and outspoken Christian around is a new Christian. His sincere faith and love for spiritual things are contagious and attractive to others who love the truth.) Hence, Paul told Timothy not to give this position to new converts for their own soul's sake regardless how well they might be received or needed to fill that office. **Such a violation on Timothy's part could stumble the new Christian to the place where he will be damned, just as the devil himself will be. (Rev. 20:10 shows the devil's end.) The word translated *judgment* in the NIV or *condemnation* in the KJV has the meaning of *damnation* and is found in Jude 4, describing the destiny of the teachers who change *grace* into a license for immorality.**

Again, it is crystal clear that Paul wrote of the possibility of loss of salvation, through the sin of pride. (Pride precedes a fall, Prov. 16:18.) **Had Paul believed in eternal security it would have been impossible for him to warn to this degree.** (Notice: If such a new Christian would be spiritually stumbled like that, it wouldn't be because he was predestined for such a sin or fall. Such a spiritual fatality could be avoided by knowledge and proper procedure.)

Apostasy in the Last Days

Passage four is:

The Spirit clearly says that in later times **some will abandon the faith and follow deceiving spirits and things taught by demons.** (1 Tim 4:1)

Only in a dark day when ignorance of the Scriptures is prevailing could so-called teachers get away with saying that one can *abandon the faith* and *never be in the faith* (as some teach) or *remain saved* (as others teach). Such is the hour in which we live. **Paul openly wanted Christians to know the real truth that *some* people, who had been washed in the blood of Jesus from their sin and received salvation, would afterwards turn and follow doctrines of demons! (The Apostle knew a true Christian could be deceived doctrinally and become heretical.)**
Note: The same Greek word translated *abandon* (NIV) or *depart* (KJV) in 1 Tim. 4:1 is also found in Luke 8:13, which also describes what **Jesus said happens to a true believer** who stops believing and consequently *falls away.*

Timothy, This is How To Save Yourself and Your Hearers

Passage five:

Watch your **life and doctrine closely.** Persevere in them, because if you do, **you will save both yourself and your hearers.** (1 Tim 4:16)

Paul stressed life (behavior) and doctrine (teaching) in his epistles and especially here in this passage. Such would be exceptionally vital for someone like Timothy, who was a preacher. By persevering in a holy life and sound teaching, Timothy would *save* himself, as well as those he would teach. This, however, is not the norm in our day. **Again, Paul taught a Christian has free will and human responsibility in his own salvation and will likewise affect others around him. (1 Tim. 4:16 is a good Scripture for all pastors and teachers to memorize.)**

Some Christian Widows Turned Away to *Follow Satan*

Passage six deals with Paul's directives for younger widows, those under sixty years of age:

So I counsel **younger widows** to marry, to have children, to manage their homes and to give the enemy no opportunity for slander. **Some have in fact already turned away to follow Satan.** (1 Tim 5:14,15)

Paul actually knew of some Christian widows that turned away from following Jesus to *follow* Satan. (Paul never even suggested that if such occurs then you can be sure *they were never saved to begin with*, as some might in our day.) It is painfully clear that the very widows that *turned away* previously had a *dedication to Christ:*

As for **younger widows,** do not put them on such a list. For when their sensual desires overcome **their dedication to Christ,** they want to marry. Thus they bring judgment on themselves, because they have broken their first pledge. (1 Tim 5:11,12)

The ones Paul knew went from *dedication to Christ* to a follower of Satan (again). **Timothy could help prevent more spiritual tragedies like that by not allowing younger Christian widows to be placed on the widow's list.** No widow was to be put on such a list unless she was over *sixty years* of age (v. 9).

A Warning to People Who Want to get *Rich*

Passage seven deals with **deadly spiritual dangers** that come from the desire to get rich:

People who **want to get rich** fall into temptation and a trap and into **many foolish and harmful desires that plunge men into ruin and destruction.** For the love of money is a root of all kinds of evil. **Some people, eager for money, have wandered from the faith** and pierced themselves with many griefs. But you, man of God, flee from all this, and pursue **righteousness, godliness, faith, love, endurance and gentleness.** (1 Tim 6:9-11)

Again, Paul mentions more sad cases. This time he refers to other former Christians he knew that *wandered* away from their salvation, because of their desire to *get rich*. (Paul knew of many people that did not stay saved, but that turned from their own salvation, apart from God's will, and got back on the road to damnation once again.)

Note: The Greek word translated *destruction* in 1 Tim. 6:9 is also found in Mt. 7:13 and refers to hell.

(1 Tim. 6:9-11 is also a primary refutation to the present day Prosperity message, another deadly but popular false teaching. Paul told Timothy to *flee* the desire to be personally rich and told him what to *pursue*, which is much more important and lasting.)

More *Wanderers* From the Faith

The eighth passage is:

Timothy, guard what has been entrusted to your care. Turn away from **godless chatter and the opposing ideas of what is falsely called knowledge**, which some have professed and in so doing have **wandered from the faith.** Grace be with you. (1 Tim 6:20, 21)

Finally, another warning of life or death magnitude is given about godless talk and teachings that are contradictory to Scripture, which could lead to the spiritual downfall of even Timothy himself, as it did for other Christians. See also 2 Tim. 2:16. He was, therefore, solemnly instructed by Paul to *turn away* from such.

Summary

As Paul fought legalism he also taught a conditional security for the believer simultaneously. **Hence, to teach against *legalism* is not to teach eternal security, like many have been deceived to think by the savage wolves themselves.** Without a doubt, Paul taught as only a conditional security teacher could. He knew many who turned from their salvation over various temptations and doctrines.

Secondly, Paul never even implied that the named or unnamed people who turned away to follow Satan, abandoned the faith, wandered away from a pure heart, good conscience and sincere faith, etc. were *never saved to begin with,* as some OSAS people would want us all to believe. In fact,

Paul stressed the opposite. Those people were previously saved and the same horrible thing can happen to any Christian, including Timothy and **you** the Christian reader. Face the facts. Paul also knew that such could happen to even himself, an apostle (1 Cor. 9:27), as it did to the Apostle Judas Iscariot.

Thirdly, a Christian's future sins are not already forgiven before he commits them, like some think. If they were, then those referred to in 1 Tim 1:5,6 could never have wandered away from a *pure* heart, which happened.

Finally, as Jesus taught about the various things that can happen to people who hear the word of God in the Parable of the Sower (Luke 8:4-15), Paul similarly mentioned many of the spiritual fatalities he was personally aware of in 1 Timothy, and elsewhere. **He wanted the disturbing, unpopular truth known, so Christian people would be more on their guard against false teachers and sin and** *keep themselves pure* **(1 Tim. 5:22) from sin's defilements. See also James 1:27b.**

Dear reader, this life for the Christian is a spiritually risky one, which is lived in a hostile environment filled with sin and deception. Don't let anyone convince you otherwise. **There are many spiritual dangers through sin and false doctrines that can stumble true Christians to the point where they lose their salvation, go back into sin as a dog returns to his vomit (2 Pet. 2:22); etc. Therefore, the Christian must** *constantly* **remain on his spiritual guard for his own salvation's sake, as well as for his effect on others. May no one who reads this ever be deceived into thinking differently, even if pseudo-scholarly persuasion would come from popular** *ear-tickling eternal security savage wolves in sheep's clothing***, who will deny and distort these precious eternal facts of the Christian life.**

6

Entrusted With The Gospel

In the well known *Parable of the Talents,* we are clearly shown that the Christian is *entrusted* **with the Lord's property and will one day give an account.** Please take a few minutes and carefully read what Jesus taught:

Again, it will be like a man going on a journey, who called his servants and **entrusted** his property to them. To one he gave five talents of money, to another two talents, and to another one talent, each according to his ability. Then he went on his journey. The man who had received the five talents went at once and put his money to work and gained five more. So also, the one with the two talents gained two more. But the man who had received the one talent went off, dug a hole in the ground and hid his master's money. After a long time the master of those servants returned and settled accounts with them. The man who had received the five talents brought the other five. "Master," he said, "you **entrusted** me with five talents. See, I have gained five more." His master replied, "Well done, good and faithful servant! You have been faithful with a few things; I will put you in charge of many things. Come and share your master's happiness!" The man with the two talents also came. "Master," he said, "you **entrusted** me with two talents; see, I have gained two more." His master replied, "Well done, good and faithful servant! You have been faithful with a few things; I will put you in charge of many things. Come and share your master's happiness!" Then the man who had received the one talent came. "Master," he said, "I knew that you are a hard man, harvesting where you have not sown and gathering where you have not scattered seed. So I was afraid and went out and hid your talent in the ground. See, here is what belongs to you." His master replied, "You wicked, lazy servant! So you knew that I harvest where I have not sown and gather where I have not scattered seed? Well then, you should have put my money on deposit with the bankers, so that when I returned I would have received it back with interest. Take the talent from him and give it to the one who has the ten talents. For everyone who has will be given more, and he will have an abundance. Whoever does not have, even what he has will be taken from him. **And throw that worthless servant outside, into the darkness, where there will be weeping and gnashing of teeth."** (Mat 25:14-30)

According to the Lord, it is a very serious act of irresponsibility not to be faithful with this trust. In fact, the seriousness of this sin of omission and neglect will cost a Christian his potential entrance into the kingdom of God. [To be thrown into the darkness where there will be weeping and gnashing of teeth is to be thrown in the *fiery furnace* (Mt. 13:42,50), another way of describing hell, where all of the wicked will be tormented.] Hence, being faithful to the Lord by being responsible in his service is of life or death in importance.

The same truth about this trust shows up at another time in regard to the Christian's judgment:

But the one who does not know and does things deserving punishment will be beaten with few blows. From everyone who has been given much, much will be demanded; and from the one who has been **entrusted** with much, much more will be asked. (Luke 12:48)

Whatever you might have thought about Judgment Day that doesn't parallel that truth, please reject it for your own good. **All Christians have been given a very serious call and valuable trust—to bring forth *gain* or be thrown into outer darkness where there is weeping and gnashing of teeth**. In light of this, have you ever considered the wasted opportunities to serve God that slip through the fingers of many who profess salvation? Dearly beloved, we are going to have to stand before God and account for these! **Now is the time to change and become what God wants before it is too late.**

Paul's Trust

What did Paul think he was *entrusted* with? Carefully ponder the following and the answer will become evident:

So then, men ought to regard us as servants of Christ and as those **entrusted** with the secret things of God. (1 Cor 4:1)

On the contrary, they saw that I had been **entrusted** with the task of preaching the gospel to the Gentiles, just as Peter had been to the Jews. (Gal 2:7)

On the contrary, we speak as men approved by God to be **entrusted** with the gospel. We are not trying to please men but God, who tests our hearts. (1 Th 2:4)

that conforms to the glorious gospel of the blessed God, which he **entrusted** to me. (1 Tim 1:11)

and at his appointed season he brought his word to light through the preaching **entrusted** to me by the command of God our Savior (Titus 1:3)

You Have Been *Entrusted* Too

You are correct if you thought Paul was entrusted with the *gospel.* No doubt some might wrongly say, "But that was Paul. He was an *apostle* unlike me so I'm not *entrusted* with spreading the gospel like he was." If that is your understanding, please readjust your thinking! Notice the following Scripture written to all of the Christians in Rome:

But thanks be to God that, though you used to be slaves to sin, you wholeheartedly obeyed the form of **teaching** to which you were **entrusted.** (Rom 6:17)

According to Rom. 6:17, all of the Christians at Rome were *entrusted* **with a teaching**. What *teaching* could this possibly be other than the *gospel,* which the Lord spoke of in the following passage:

Then Jesus came to them and said, "All authority in heaven and on earth has been given to me. Therefore go and make disciples of all nations, baptizing them in the name of the Father and of the Son and of the Holy Spirit, and **teaching them to obey everything I have commanded you.** And surely I am with you always, to the very end of the age." (Mat 28:18-20)

After Jesus' resurrection from the dead, he commissioned the Eleven (the Twelve apostles minus Judas) to *go* and make disciples, then water baptize them and teach them to *obey everything* they themselves were commanded to do, which directly includes **spreading the gospel.** This both clarifies and supplements Rom. 6:17 regarding the *teaching* all saints are *entrusted* with. In other words, as the Eleven were *entrusted* with the gospel message, all other Christians are too. Or we might say it this way: **As with Paul, all Christians with no exceptions have been given this same awesome responsibility of spreading the gospel, but few seem to be doing anything about it, to the detriment of other precious souls, as well as their own.**

The *Faith* Has Been Entrusted To The Saints

Another Scripture which reflects what Christians have been *entrusted* with is found in the following:

Dear friends, although I was very eager to write to you about the salvation we share, I felt I had to write and urge you to contend for the faith that was once for all **entrusted** to the saints. (Jude 3)

Here *the faith* is what has been *entrusted* to the saints. This includes you, if you are a real Christian. According to the very next verse we learn that the Jude 3 command is connected with *grace:*

For certain men whose condemnation was written about long ago have secretly slipped in among you. They are godless men, who change the **grace** of our God into a license for immorality and deny Jesus Christ our only Sovereign and Lord. (Jude 4)

The urgent message declared by Jude was about false teachers who distorted the message of *grace* into something very different—*a license for immorality*. (**The true grace of God teaches holy living, Titus 2:12.**) Hence, the urgent call for early Christians, as well as all in our day, is to *contend* for the true faith against the counterfeit *grace* teachings. That Greek word *contend* comes from two words, one of which means the following:

> *agonizomai*, ag-o-nid'-zom-ahee; from G73; to struggle, lit. (to compete for a prize), fig. (**to contend with an adversary**), or gen. (to endeavor to accomplish something):—**fight, labor fervently, strive.**

If you are a real Christian, you are to get very serious about this trust you have been given as cited in Jude 3,4. It is a trust, which God will hold you accountable for, according to the *Parable of the Talents*.

In our day, the eternal security wolves have been wrongly exalted as great teachers of God's word, but the truth is: Christians are given a command to *labor fervently* against their dangerous version of grace. The Christian's life is a *battle* for truth and souls—your own soul, as well as others. Not to battle against the eternal security grace twisters will allow their poisonous message to spread more freely. We are to *warn* the righteous man about sin, as well as the wicked:

> When I say to a wicked man, "You will surely die," and you do not warn him or speak out to dissuade him from his evil ways in order to save his life, that wicked man will die for his sin, and I will hold you accountable for his blood. But if you do warn the wicked man and he does not turn from his wickedness or from his evil ways, he will die for his sin; but you will have saved yourself. Again, when a **righteous** man turns from his righteousness and does evil, and I put a stumbling block before him, he will die. Since you did not **warn** him, he will die for his sin. The **righteous** things he did will not be remembered, and I will hold you accountable for his blood. But if you do **warn** the **righteous** man not to sin and he does not sin, he will surely live because he took warning, and you will have saved yourself. (Ezek 3:18-21)

The Real Gospel

As in the days of the Apostle Paul, there is *another gospel* being spread in our day (Gal. 1:6-9). This counterfeit being proclaimed by well-known teachers is not the same as Paul's gospel of grace:

Now, brothers, I want to remind you of **the gospel I preached to you,** which you received and on which you have taken your stand. **By this gospel you are saved, if you hold firmly to the word I preached to you. Otherwise, you have believed in vain.** For what I received I passed on to you as of first importance: that Christ died for our sins according to the Scriptures, that he was buried, that he was raised on the third day according to the Scriptures, (1 Cor 15:1-4)

Once you were alienated from God and were enemies in your minds because of your evil behavior. But now he has reconciled you by Christ's physical body through death to present you holy in his sight, without blemish and free from accusation—**if you continue in your faith,** established and firm, not moved from the hope held out in the gospel. **This is the gospel** that you heard and that has been proclaimed to every creature under heaven, and of which I, Paul, have become a servant. (Col 1:21-23)

I am not ashamed of the gospel, because it is the power of God for the salvation of everyone who believes: first for the Jew, then for the Gentile. For **in the gospel** a righteousness from God is revealed, a righteousness that is by faith from first to last, just as it is written: "The righteous will live by faith." (Rom 1:16,17)

Remember Jesus Christ, raised from the dead, descended from David. This is my **gospel** (2 Tim 2:8)

According to those Scriptures we know the following about the real gospel, *entrusted* to Paul and all Christians: It is the plan of salvation centering around Jesus' death, burial and resurrection, in which a righteousness by faith is revealed. But that is not all. The real gospel includes a **conditional security for the Christian, according to the real grace teacher. Notice again what he wrote about the** *gospel:*

By this **gospel** you are saved, **if you hold firmly to the word I preached to you. Otherwise, you have believed in vain.** (1 Cor 15:2)

If you continue in your faith, established and firm, not moved from the hope held out in the **gospel.** This is the **gospel** that you heard and that has been proclaimed to every creature under heaven, and of which I, Paul, have become a servant. (Col 1:23)

Also, the real gospel clearly excludes the *immoral, impure, greedy, sinful* and *unholy* from salvation:

For of this you can be sure: No immoral, impure or greedy person—such a man is an idolater—has any inheritance in the kingdom of Christ and of God. Let no one deceive you with empty words, for because of such things God's wrath comes on those who are disobedient. Therefore do not be partners with them. (Eph 5:5-7)

We also know that law is made not for the righteous but for lawbreakers and rebels, the ungodly and **sinful, the unholy** and irreligious; for those who kill their fathers or mothers, for murderers, for adulterers and perverts, for slave traders and liars and perjurers—and for whatever else is contrary to the sound doctrine that **conforms to the glorious gospel of the blessed God, which he entrusted to me.** (1 Tim 1:9-11)

According to the counterfeit gospel of eternal security, the immoral, impure, greedy, sinful and unholy, if ever saved, will still have salvation in contrast to the real *gospel* message.

The True *Gospel* is Supremely Exalted

Jesus actually exalted the one-and-only message which brings salvation, called the *gospel*, on a par with himself in the following passages!

For whoever wants to save his life will lose it, but whoever loses his life for **me** and for the **gospel** will save it. (Mark 8:35)

"I tell you the truth," Jesus replied, "no one who has left home or brothers or sisters or mother or father or children or fields for **me** and the **gospel** will fail to receive a hundred times as much in this present age (homes, brothers, sisters, mothers, children and fields—and with them, persecutions) and **in the age to come, eternal life**." (Mark 10: 29,30)

Why is the *Gospel* Message so Exalted?

The gospel is a unique one-of-a-kind message of *good news*. It is so highly valued and precious because it alone can bring salvation to those who receive it. Since *salvation* itself is so awesomely important, then the message that brings it about is of equal importance. (It is not surprising then that the devil would have various counterfeit "gospels" to confuse and discourage people in coming to God or even staying with him after they find salvation.)

Notice the following that resulted from the real gospel going forth by Paul:

Even though you have ten thousand guardians in Christ, you do not have many fathers, **for in Christ Jesus I became your father through the gospel.** (1 Cor 4:15)

Paul became their spiritual father through the gospel message. Then we have Peter declaring the following:

After much discussion, Peter got up and addressed them: "Brothers, you know that some time ago God made a choice among you that **the Gentiles might hear from my lips the message of the gospel and believe.**" (Acts 15:7)

Peter spoke that Scripture regarding what happened when he delivered the gospel to Cornelius. See Acts 10:43-48. The result was they got their sins forgiven. (That occurred before and without water baptism!)

Both of these Scriptures are actually in fulfillment to what Jesus said would happen, that is, people saved in the future would come to *believe* on himself through a message (the *gospel*):

My prayer is not for them alone. I pray also for **those who will be-** **lieve in me through their message.** (John 17:20)

So the only way to enter heaven and escape hell fire is through the salvation found in Jesus Christ, and that salvation comes about by hearing the message of the *gospel.* Hence, the *gospel* is the most valued message which Christians have been *entrusted* with.

Eternal Security

The Christian's free will and human responsibility after initial salvation is to *hold firmly* **to the word or** *believe in vain* **(1 Cor. 15:2). This is the original** *gospel of grace,* which has been twisted and distorted into something very dangerously different, as it was in Jude's day. Today these false teachers are called **eternal security teachers.** Such have taught a license for immorality under their version of *grace* for so long and without adequate challenge it has now been widely accepted as *gospel* truth! Their false gospel has so saturated the established so-called *church* of our hour that even denominational churches that are to stand opposed to this teaching are openly teaching it to the harm of all who will accept it. This is irrefutable evidence that we are in a deep, dark apostasy.

What Are You Doing?

Dear saint, what are you personally doing to: (1) combat or *contend against* the counterfeit gospel of eternal security that is nothing more than a false hope and lie from the devil and (2) spread the genuine *gospel,* which is still hated in our day as it was in Paul's? Please, for the sake of souls take these commands seriously. There is much more you can be doing regarding your Christian responsibilities. Earnestly seek the Lord and ponder your own situation to recognize more that you can do.

[Since the word of God sometimes *closes* eyes (Isa. 6:10) as well as *opening* them (Acts 26:18), we cannot correctly interpret the *gain* in the *Parable of the Talents* to always mean new converts. **While it certainly includes converts, it can also include other things as well.**]

The Pastor's Trust

As serious as all of that is, it is even magnified for pastors. Notice the following:

Timothy, guard what has been **entrusted** to your care. Turn away from godless chatter and the opposing ideas of what is falsely called knowledge (1 Tim 6:20)

Guard the good deposit that was **entrusted** to you—guard it with the help of the Holy Spirit who lives in us. (2 Tim 1:14)

Since an overseer is **entrusted** with God's work, he must be blameless—not overbearing, not quick-tempered, not given to drunkenness, not violent, not pursuing dishonest gain. (Titus 1:7)

Even though you have ten thousand **guardians** in Christ, you do not have many fathers, for in Christ Jesus I became your father through the gospel. (1 Cor 4:15)

A pastor or shepherd is to be a *guardian* of the sheep they are to watch over:

Obey your leaders and submit to their authority. They keep **watch over** you as men who must give an account. Obey them so that their work will be a joy, not a burden, for that would be of no advantage to you. (Heb 13:17)

But at the same time, the following also applies to pastors:

Not lording it over those **entrusted** to you, but being examples to the flock. (1 Pet 5:3)

So a pastor's trust is with the gospel message itself, as well as the people who sit under his spiritual care. Notice the following directive about final salvation for the pastor and the souls entrusted to his care:

Watch your life and doctrine closely. Persevere in them, because **if you do, you will save both yourself and your hearers**. (1 Tim 4:16)

All teachers will have a more strict judgment, including a pastor:

> Not many of you should presume to be teachers, my brothers, because you know that **we who teach will be judged more strictly.** (James 3:1)

Hence, teaching is to be reserved for reliable men, sound in doctrine and who are living holy. See Titus 1:6-9 and 1 Tim. 3:2-7. This is so because their influence will affect all who hear them.

Mini-Sermons

Why then are so many pastors preaching mini-sermons that are filled with stories, jokes, psychology and other things rather than the *word of God,* which they are to preach (2 Tim. 4:2-4)? Whatever the reason is, no doubt many pastors need to **repent** and start taking their responsibilities much more seriously since eternal souls are at stake, including their own! **If the hours wasted in front of the TV and reading joke books were spent in the Bible and prayer, the sheep might be fed something wholesome instead of a burnt, dried, spiritual bread crumb that can't build anyone up spiritually.** The sheep are starving to death in the churches for lack of wholesome, spiritual food, while the pastors are going golfing, vacationing, seeking entertainment and amusements! (If you are a pastor and this is describing you—stop at this moment and wholeheartedly repent before Almighty God and return to your *first love.*)

Your Time, Money, Knowledge and God-Given Abilities

As for Christians who are not pastors, please know that your **time, money, knowledge, abilities** and everything else you have—all of which has been given to you by God, will have to be accounted for. It is time to get zealous as well as deadly serious in this **battle for eternity**, which will mean drastic changes for many:

> Never be lacking in zeal, but keep your spiritual fervor, serving the Lord. (Rom 12:11)

> Only let us live up to what we have already **attained**. (Phil 3:16)

However, I consider my life worth nothing to me, **if only I may finish the race and complete the task the Lord Jesus has given me—the task of testifying to the gospel of God's grace.** (Acts 20:24)

7

Which Gospel Or Salvation Do You Believe?

Among people who call themselves Bible-believing, born again Christians there are primarily two different salvation messages (*gospels*) that are proclaimed. **The gospel associated with eternal security would have you believe that:**

■ Salvation begins in a moment's time and is guaranteed to continue.
■ There is no salvation maintenance on man's part. God will keep you, hold you and has already sealed you by His Spirit at the point of salvation assuring an entrance into the kingdom of heaven.
■ Sin can never bring a Christian to his spiritual death, regardless what sin is committed or false doctrine is believed.
■ Eternal life is a gift that can't be lost or returned and a present tense possession for the Christian, guaranteeing an entrance into God's kingdom.
■ Reaching heaven for the Christian is absolutely certain just as though he has already been in heaven for 10,000 years.
■ Some Christians are adulterers, drunkards, thieves, etc.

In contrast, **the real *gospel* which rejects eternal security** states that:

■ Salvation begins in a moment's time and continues on, but only as long as we follow Jesus. This implies the possibility that something can adversely interfere with it, as has happened in the lives of Solomon, Saul, Judas and many others.

■ After getting born again (initial salvation) there is salvation maintenance **on man's part**, which is under Biblical *grace*. If this is ne-
glected, the Christian will inevitably drift away, turn lukewarm, grow
unfruitful, become unloving and unforgiving as well as regress spiritually in other ways to the point that spiritual life is no longer present
within his spirit. Man cooperates with God and enables Him to keep
and hold us spiritually safe. Though God is sovereign, He will never
violate man's free will, even if it is to man's detriment and damnation. Christians can put to death the misdeeds of the sinful nature
(flesh) by the Spirit of God—never by their own ability or strength.

■ Sin can defile, corrupt, contaminate, soil and even bring the Christian
to his spiritual death. The seal of the Holy Spirit can be broken. Consequently, we must be on our spiritual guard at all times, as we look
to God for his strength and power. The Christian life is a war, fight
and struggle against the deceiving forces of darkness and personal
sin.

■ Eternal life is much more than just a gift and a present tense possession. It is also a hope (Titus 3:7) and promise (1 Jn. 2:24,25), yet to
be reaped (Gal. 6:8,9), in the age to come (Mk. 10:30), but only for
those who persist in doing good (Rom. 2:7) and who don't grow
weary and give up sowing to please the Spirit of God and not the sinful nature (Gal. 6:8,9).

■ The only salvation assurance the Bible offers is a present tense salvation assurance for the person who is presently following Jesus and
trusting in Him for his own personal salvation (1 Jn. 5:11-13). In
other words, the faith needed to enter God's paradise kingdom is a
trusting, submitting and **enduring** faith. To enter God's kingdom, we
must endure hardships and persecutions as we continue to live holy
as Jesus' disciples in this wicked and adulterous generation. Sadly,
continuing in the faith and holiness has not always happened for
others in times past.

■ It is impossible to be a Christian at the same time as being an adulterer, drunkard, thief, or such as is cited in 1 Cor. 6:9,10; Rev. 21:8;
Eph. 5:5-7; Mk. 7:20-22. To teach that such is possible is to twist the
holy image of being a Christian (a *saint*) into something which allows
for wickedness. Eternal security is a dangerous myth, which has
many on the road to hell thinking they are on the road to heaven
because they once had a moment of true faith which brought regen-

eration. Please see our book, *The Believer's Conditional Security* for much more information.

The gospel based on eternal security is built upon partial truths presented as the whole truth and various Scriptural distortions, as well as misrepresenting the true Christian gospel and grace. Jude was adamant and clear in his epistle about those who change grace into a license for immorality. He said they are godless people, who don't have the Spirit of God and for whom blackest darkness has been prepared. Paul stated that to preach a false gospel (another gospel) is cause enough for eternal condemnation. OSAS doctrine is a false gospel, as well as a heresy.

8

Taking The Scissors To 1 Cor. 15:2

Without doubt, sometimes it's advantageous to use ellipses (...), which indicate an omitted part from a quoted statement. This is often a legitimate means of written communication. However, through an ellipsis, sometimes information vital and relevant to the context can be cleverly concealed!

I've noticed when the eternal security teachers refer to the gospel from 1 Cor. 15:1-4, they often make a point of avoiding verse 2! They usually do this by starting to read or write at verse 3 and just mentioning, in passing, the subject of Paul's gospel from verse 1.[1] Sometimes, however, the omission of verse 2 is much more obvious, but only to those who know what that verse says or to those who will spend the time to check the reference and read it from the Bible for themselves! One example of this exact kind of omission by an eternal security teacher is the following:

> For example, in Ephesians 2:8-9 the Apostle Paul declared, "For by grace are ye saved through faith; and that not of yourselves, it is the gift of God Not of works, lest any man should boast." Paul also identified the specific Word of God in which people of this present age must believe in order to be saved. That Word is the gospel defined in 1 Corinthians 15:1-4: "I declare unto you the gospel which I preached unto you, which also ye have received and in which ye stand; By which also ye are saved . . . that Christ died for our sins

---

1   David Breese did this in his tracts: *Heaven And How To Get There* and *The Assurance Of Salvation*.

according to the scriptures; And that he was buried, and that he rose again the third day according to the scriptures."[2]

What are the missing words, as indicated by the three dots? They are most of verse 2 and part of verse 3, as quoted in the King James Bible as follows:

If ye keep in memory what I preached unto you, **unless ye have believed in vain**. For I declared unto you first of all that which I also received, how

Why do you suppose those clear and powerful words from verse 2 were omitted? Do they affect the statement being quoted by their omission? Though we can't answer the "why" question, we can the second. Certainly, the omitted words from verse 2 clearly teach the believer's security is **conditional** and not unconditional as Dr. Showers embraces as true. Showers cut short verse 2 immediately before the conditional word "if" is stated, thereby making the statement seem unconditional instead of conditional! Reader, can you see how this completely changes the original statement by the Apostle Paul? If you made the statement: "Interstate 70 will lead you to Denver, Colorado in ten hours, if you don't stop too many times" and someone later quoted you, omitting the latter part of that statement which begins with the word "if," it would be a distortion! This is similar to what the eternal security teachers often do with 1 Cor. 15:2.

Please note, Paul used all those words in verse 2 to explain his gospel of grace. By these words, Paul clearly stated that in his gospel, the believer's security was **conditional even before** he mentioned the death, burial and resurrection of Christ in verses 3 and 4. Though the eternal security adherents hate this fact, they can't refute it! See also Rom. 11:19-23 and Col. 1:23, two other Pauline passages which also show the believer's security is conditional.

Beloved, remember the whole truth is vital regardless how disturbing or unpopular that truth may be!

9

Is A Christian A Sinner?

We have received many emails over the years either stating that *all Christians are sinners* or that they *must continue to sin all the time in this life*. This chapter is written for the express purpose of shedding Biblical light on this subject. The reader is asked to drop all preconceived ideas about this and ponder the various times the words *sinner* and *sinners* are found in the Bible. Cited in this chapter is **every verse that contains these words in the New Testament**. After this list, several important observations will be made as a consequence:

And there was a woman in the city who was a **sinner**; and when she learned that He was reclining *at the table* in the Pharisee's house, she brought an alabaster vial of perfume. (Luke 7:37)

Now when the Pharisee who had invited Him saw this, he said to himself, "If this man were a prophet He would know who and what sort of person this woman is who is touching Him, that she is a **sinner**." (Luke 7:39)

I tell you that in the same way, there will be *more* joy in heaven over one **sinner** who repents than over ninety-nine righteous persons who need no repentance. (Luke 15:7)

In the same way, I tell you, there is joy in the presence of the angels of God over one **sinner** who repents. (Luke 15:10)

But the tax collector, standing some distance away, was even unwilling to lift up his eyes to heaven, but was beating his breast, saying, "God, be merciful to me, the **sinner!**" (Luke 18:13)

When they saw it, they all *began* to grumble, saying, "He has gone to be the guest of a man who is a **sinner.**" (Luke 19:7)

Therefore some of the Pharisees were saying, "This man is not from God, because He does not keep the Sabbath." But others were saying, "How can a man who is a **sinner** perform such signs?" And there was a division among them. (John 9:16)

So a second time they called the man who had been blind, and said to him, "Give glory to God; we know that this man is a **sinner.**" (John 9:24)

He then answered, "Whether He is a **sinner**, I do not know; one thing I do know, that though I was blind, now I see." (John 9:25)

Someone might argue, "If my falsehood enhances God's truthfulness and so increases his glory, why am I still condemned as a **sinner**?" (Rom 3:7)

let him know that he who turns a **sinner** from the error of his way will save his soul from death and will cover a multitude of sins. (Jam 5:20)

And if it is with difficulty that the righteous is saved, what will become of the godless man and the **sinner?** (1 Pet 4:18)

Then it happened that as Jesus was reclining *at the table* in the house, behold, many tax collectors and **sinners** came and were dining with Jesus and His disciples. (Mat 9:10)

When the Pharisees saw *this*, they said to His disciples, "Why is your Teacher eating with the tax collectors and **sinners**?" (Mat 9:11)

But go and learn what this means: "I desire compassion, and not sacrifice," for I did not come to call the righteous, but **sinners**. (Mat 9:13)

The Son of Man came eating and drinking, and they say, "Behold, a gluttonous man and a drunkard, a friend of tax collectors and **sinners**!" Yet wisdom is vindicated by her deeds. (Mat 11:19)

Then He came to the disciples and said to them, "Are you still sleeping and resting? Behold, the hour is at hand and the Son of Man is being betrayed into the hands of **sinners**." (Mat 26:45)

And it happened that He was reclining *at the table* in his house, and many tax collectors and **sinners** were dining with Jesus and His disciples; for there were many of them, and they were following Him. (Mark 2:15)

When the scribes of the Pharisees saw that He was eating with the **sinners** and tax collectors, they said to His disciples, "Why is He eating and drinking with tax collectors and **sinners**?" (Mark 2:16) And hearing *this*, Jesus said to them, "*it is* not those who are healthy who need a physician, but those who are sick; I did not come to call the righteous, but **sinners**." (Mark 2:17)

And He came the third time, and said to them, "Are you still sleeping and resting? It is enough; the hour has come; behold, the Son of Man is being betrayed into the hands of **sinners**." (Mark 14:41)

The Pharisees and their scribes *began* grumbling at His disciples, saying, "Why do you eat and drink with the tax collectors and **sinners**?" (Luke 5:30)

I have not come to call the righteous but **sinners** to repentance. (Luke 5:32)

If you love those who love you, what credit is *that* to you? For even **sinners** love those who love them. (Luke 6:32)

If you do good to those who do good to you, what credit is *that* to you? For even **sinners** do the same. (Luke 6:33)

If you lend to those from whom you expect to receive, what credit is *that* to you? Even **sinners** lend to **sinners** in order to receive back the same *amount*. (Luke 6:34)

The Son of Man has come eating and drinking, and you say, "Behold, a gluttonous man and a drunkard, a friend of tax collectors and **sinners**!" (Luke 7:34)

And Jesus said to them, "Do you suppose that these Galileans were *greater* **sinners** than all *other* Galileans because they suffered this *fate*?" (Luke 13:2)

Now all the tax collectors and the **sinners** were coming near Him to listen to Him. (Luke 15:1)

Both the Pharisees and the scribes *began* to grumble, saying, "This man receives **sinners** and eats with them." (Luke 15:2)

We know that God does not hear **sinners**; but if anyone is God-fearing and does His will, He hears him. (John 9:31)

But God demonstrates His own love toward us, in that while we were yet **sinners**, Christ died for us. (Rom 5:8)

For as through the one man's disobedience the many were made **sinners**, even so through the obedience of the One the many will be made righteous. (Rom 5:19)

We *are* Jews by nature and not **sinners** from among the Gentiles. (Gal 2:15)

But if, while seeking to be justified in Christ, we ourselves have also been found **sinners**, is Christ then a minister of sin? May it never be! (Gal 2:17) realizing the fact that law is not made for a righteous person, but for those who are lawless and rebellious, for the ungodly and **sinners**, for the unholy and profane, for those who kill their fathers or mothers, for murderers. (1 Tim 1:9)

For it was fitting for us to have such a high priest, holy, innocent, undefiled, separated from **sinners** and exalted above the heavens. (Heb 7:26)

For consider Him who has endured such hostility by **sinners** against Himself, so that you will not grow weary and lose heart. (Heb 12:3)

Draw near to God and He will draw near to you. Cleanse your hands, you **sinners**; and purify your hearts, you double-minded. (Jam 4:8)

to execute judgment upon all, and to convict all the ungodly of all their ungodly deeds which they have done in an ungodly way, and of all the harsh things which ungodly **sinners** have spoken against Him. (Jude 15)

Was Paul a *Sinner* or *Saint*?

Just listed was every verse in the New Testament where the words *sinner* or *sinners*, are found with only the following exception:

It is a trustworthy statement, deserving full acceptance, that Christ Jesus came into the world to save **sinners**, among whom I am foremost *of all*. (1 Tim 1:15)

The Apostle Paul identified himself as a *sinner* there but the context reveals **he was talking about his life *before* he came to salvation**. Notice the context of that Scripture:

I thank Christ Jesus our Lord, who has strengthened me, because He considered me faithful, putting me into service, even though **I was formerly a blasphemer and a persecutor and a violent aggressor**. Yet I was shown mercy because **I acted ignorantly in unbelief**; and the grace of our Lord was more than abundant, with the faith and love which are *found* in Christ Jesus. It is a trustworthy statement, deserving full acceptance, that Christ Jesus came into the world to save **sinners**, among whom **I am foremost** *of all*. Yet for this reason I found mercy, so that in me as the foremost, Jesus Christ might demonstrate His perfect patience as an example for those who would believe in Him for eternal life (1 Tim. 1:12-16).

When Paul wrote *I was formerly a blasphemer and a persecutor and a violent aggressor* **it clearly shows he is writing about the time when he was unsaved. This is further shown when he also wrote** *I acted ignorantly in unbelief.* How sad it is that some will remove 1 Tim. 1:15 from its context in an attempt to pin the label of *sinner* on Paul after his salvation! (See our other materials also answering their similar misrepresentation of him at Rom. 7:14-20.) What a horrible distortion of God's holy word. **This is what the eternal security teachers, especially, have done. It is nothing for them to slander the holy character of Paul in this way, or mishandle any other Scripture, as long as they can somehow portray the Christian life as allowing for wickedness, fruitlessness, worldliness and the like. The eternal security teachers have a dangerously darkened understanding of what God's word teaches and have corrupted multitudes by their teachings.**

Sinner—Repent!

Regarding the words *sinner* (or *sinners*) the truth is if you are such, then **Jesus has called you to** *repent* **(turn from wickedness):**

I have not come to call the righteous but **sinners to repentance**. (Luke 5:32)

It is crystal clear that God's word contrasts *sinners* with *righteous* people numerous times. In other words, if you are a *sinner*, then you are not *righteous* and therefore not in line for God's *kingdom*, but instead headed for *the furnace of fire*, where there will be *weeping and gnashing of teeth*:

These will go away into eternal punishment, but the **righteous into eternal life**. (Mat 25:46)

So it will be at the end of the age; the angels will come forth and take out the **wicked** from among the righteous, and will throw them **into**

the furnace of fire; in that place there will be weeping and gnashing of teeth. (Mat 13:49,50)

The Son of Man will send forth His angels, and they will gather out of His kingdom all stumbling blocks, and those who commit lawlessness, and will throw them into the furnace of fire; in that place there will be weeping and gnashing of teeth. Then **the righteous will shine forth as the sun** in the kingdom of their Father. He who has ears, let him hear. (Mat 13:41-43)

Are you *of the Devil?*

Furthermore, the one who practices sin is *of the devil*. Such a person is not considered righteous merely because of a past moment of faith as some have been deceived into believing:

Little children, make sure no one deceives you; the one who practices righteousness is **righteous**, just as He is **righteous**; the one who practices sin is of the devil; for the devil has sinned from the beginning. The Son of God appeared for this purpose, to destroy the works of the devil. (1 John 3:7,8)

Finally, Paul wrote of himself:

... there shall certainly be a resurrection of both the **righteous** and the wicked. In view of this, I also do my best to maintain **always** a blameless conscience *both* before God and before men. (Acts 24:15, 16)

Dear reader, Paul always maintained a clear conscience before God and man in light of a resurrection of both the righteous and wicked (or *sinner*). **He clearly put himself with the group that is described in Acts 24:15,16 as *righteous*. Therefore, in light of this Scripture and the aforementioned ones, neither is the Apostle Paul nor any Christian a *sinner*, even though the people who change *grace into a license for immorality* (Jude 3,4) would like you to think otherwise. By this type of misrepresenting the Christian as a *sinner*, false teachers have tainted the holy image of Christianity itself.**

10

Eternal Security And Lifestyle Sinning

Eternal security proponents often miss the clarity of Rev. 21:8, but perhaps this is what they want to do, for the sake of their doctrine. The context of that Scripture is powerfully clear and it refutes eternal security. It states:

> But the cowardly, the unbelieving, the vile, the murderers, the sexually immoral, those who practice magic arts, the idolaters and all liars—**their place will be in the fiery lake of burning sulfur.** This is the second death.

Then we have 1 Cor. 10:7 which proves that Paul's grace message declared that **a true Christian could become an** *idolater,* the same Greek word as found in Rev. 21:8. Hence, the Lord's apostles taught a person once saved could go to the lake of fire by committing this sin, since those cited in Rev. 21:8 go to the lake of fire. This alone refutes the license for immorality called "eternal security." (End of debate.)

Moreover, the 1 Cor. 10:7 passage refers back to the Golden Calf incident (cf. Ex. 32), and proves that *idolatry* **doesn't have to be habitual** *lifestyle* **to make the Corinthian Christians** *idolaters*! Again, since 1 Cor. 10:7 refers back to just **one act,** apparently **Paul believed that just one act would make the Corinthian Christians** *idolaters*!

The above truth is very similar to the fact that **it only takes one act of murder or adultery (not many) to be a Bible-defined** *murderer* **or** *adulterer,* according to Scripture:

If a man strikes someone with an iron object so that he dies, he is a murderer; the murderer shall be put to death. Or if anyone has a stone in his hand that could kill, and he strikes someone so that he dies, **he is a murderer**; the murderer shall be put to death. Or if anyone has a wooden object in his hand that could kill, and he hits someone so that he dies, he is a murderer; the murderer shall be put to death. (Num 35:16-18)

If a man commits adultery with another man's wife—with the wife of his neighbor—both **the adulterer and the adulteress** must be put to death. (Lev 20:10)

To say that a Christian can commit adultery and not be an *adulterer* is **to teach both a deadly lie and a license for immorality at the same time, even though you might claim to reject eternal security! Note: it only takes one act of murder or adultery to be a bible-defined *murderer* or *adulterer*, according to scripture.** It does not take habitual acts or *lifestyle*, as some people falsely claim. That truth is also a death blow to the eternal security sin gospel, for it **condemns David after his salvation to the lake of fire, before he repented.** David committed one act of adultery and murder and therefore was both an adulterer and murderer, according to Scripture. Even though false teachers hate this fact of Scripture, it proves that **David lost his salvation for a time!** (See pages 366-369 in *The Believer's Conditional Security* for a further explanation about David losing his salvation.)

At this point the die-hard eternal security advocates try to somehow distort these truths or cloud this issue for the sake of their doctrine which implies that all believers can turn to the wickedness of adultery and murder, like David, and remain saved, since it wasn't "lifestyle." It should be apparent at this point why eternal security is a license for immorality under the banner of grace (Jude 3,4) and **one of the greatest threats to holy living.** (NOTE: Calvinism claims the 5 points of Calvinism are *the doctrines of grace!*)

The Calvinist argument of *lifestyle* has deceived some, but not those who have pondered the above truths. Furthermore, **Paul, who wrote Gal. 5:19-21, apparently believed the Christians in the region of Galatia could sin habitually, and therefore, not inherit the kingdom of God!** Paul knew a true believer could turn away and never return. This truth is exemplified by **King Saul in the Old Testament, who totally and finally**

fell away from the faith. We must understand 1 John 3:9 and Mt. 7:23 with these facts and other such Scriptures in mind.

Remember Paul's gospel of grace and what it taught about the believer's security:

> By this gospel you are saved, **if you hold firmly to the word I preached to you. Otherwise, you have believed in vain.** (1 Cor 15:2)

> But now he has reconciled you by Christ's physical body through death to present you holy in his sight, without blemish and free from accusation—**if you continue in your faith,** established and firm, not moved from the hope held out in the gospel. This is the gospel that you heard and that has been proclaimed to every creature under heaven, and of which I, Paul, have become a servant. (Col 1:22,23)

> You will say then, "Branches were broken off so that I could be grafted in." Granted. But they were broken off because of unbelief, and you stand by faith. **Do not be arrogant, but be afraid. For if God did not spare the natural branches, he will not spare you either.** Consider therefore the kindness and sternness of God: sternness to those who fell, but kindness to you, **provided that you continue in his kindness. Otherwise, you also will be cut off.** And if they do not persist in unbelief, they will be grafted in, for God is able to graft them in again. (Rom 11:19-23)

> **Do you not know that the wicked will not inherit the kingdom of God? Do not be deceived:** Neither the sexually immoral nor idolaters nor adulterers nor male prostitutes nor homosexuals nor thieves nor the greedy nor drunkards nor slanderers nor swindlers will inherit the kingdom of God. (1 Cor 6:9,10)

Again: one does not have to commit "lifestyle" sin to be indicted by Rev. 21:8. As David did, any true believer can also lose his salvation by sinning. **Do not be deceived!**

11

Can Salvation Be Lost With One Sin?

Over the years as I have *contended* for the faith against eternal security (Jude 3,4), I have met some people who say they reject eternal security, but then teach a Christian can engage in *occasional* acts of adultery, drunkenness, theft, etc. and remain saved. Such usually deny that David lost his salvation when in unrepentant adultery and murder. Others have said it is possible to lose your salvation, but it is *very hard* to do so. One even stated that *you must tell God that you don't want him* before you'll lose your salvation. It is the purpose of this chapter to examine the Biblical evidence for these claims to see if they have validity and to ascertain if Scripture states salvation can be lost with a single act of certain kinds of sin. (Please know that **all sin is not of the same degree**—some leads to *death* while others don't, 1 John 5:16,17.)

How many times must a righteous person sin in order to lose his salvation? Must it be *lifestyle* or *continuous* sinning? Does one have to *practice* sin before he becomes unsaved or shows himself *never saved to begin with*, as some would say? Let's look at God's word.

The Eternal Facts

A true *grace* teacher declared:

> Or do you not know that the unrighteous will not inherit the kingdom of God? Do not be deceived; neither **fornicators**, nor **idolaters**, nor **adulterers**, nor **effeminate**, nor **homosexuals**, nor **thieves**, nor *the*

65

covetous, nor **drunkards**, nor **revilers**, nor **swindlers**, will inherit the kingdom of God (1 Cor. 6:9,10, NASB).

According to the above Scripture, if any person is described there he will not inherit the kingdom of God. **So how hard is it to become a bible-defined *adulterer* or any of the others in the list?** Must a person *practice* adultery before he becomes a bible-defined **adulterer**? Must it be *lifestyle*? Here are the facts:

If a man commits adultery with another man's wife—with the wife of his neighbor—both the **adulterer** and the adulteress must be put to death. (Lev 20:10)

As just shown, God's word is consistent with the definition of the word *adulterer*—one who commits adultery. Hence, any person who commits one or more acts of adultery is an *adulterer*. The same can likewise be said about the other words bolded in 1 Cor. 6:9,10. The definition is **one who commits that particular act**, whether it is stealing, drunkenness, idolatry, etc. It doesn't have to be 5, 16, or 113 times or the nebulous *lifestyle* before they become a fornicator, idolater, adulterer, effeminate, homosexual, thief, covetous, drunkard, reviler or swindler of 1 Cor. 6:9,10. This is crystal clear, as shown above, with the word *adulterer*.

It Doesn't Have To Be *Continual* or *Lifestyle* Sinning

Other Scriptures reveal the same devastating truth, refuting the idea that *continual* or *lifestyle* sinning is the only way to lose salvation (or show one was *never really saved*). For example:

If a man strikes someone with an iron object so that he dies, he is a **murderer**; the murderer shall be put to death. (Num 35:16)

Again, a single act of *murder* makes a person a *murderer*. (That would include suicides, who are self-murderers.) Such a single act of sin will exclude any person from God's kingdom, unless he repents:

But the cowardly, the unbelieving, the vile, the **murderers**, the sexually immoral, those who practice magic arts, the idolaters and all liars—**their place will be in the fiery lake of burning sulfur.** This is the second death. (Rev 21:8)

Disowning Jesus

The Lord Jesus told those already saved the following:

But whoever disowns me before men, I will disown him before my Father in heaven. (Mat 10:33)

Later we learn that all of the original apostles, except Judas who betrayed Jesus, *disowned* the Lord:

Then Jesus told them, "This very night you will all fall away on account of me, for it is written: 'I will strike the shepherd, and the sheep of the flock will be scattered.' But after I have risen, I will go ahead of you into Galilee." Peter replied, "Even if all fall away on account of you, I never will." "I tell you the truth," Jesus answered, "this very night, before the rooster crows, **you will disown me three times.**" But Peter declared, "Even if I have to die with you, I will never disown you." And all the other disciples said the same. (Mat 26:31-35)

So how hard was it for Peter to *disown* Jesus and *fall away*? It wasn't very hard and occurred in a **short period of time:**

Now Peter was sitting out in the courtyard, and a servant girl came to him. **"You also were with Jesus of Galilee,"** she said. **But he denied it before them all. "I don't know what you're talking about," he said.** Then he went out to the gateway, where another girl saw him and said to the people there, **"This fellow was with Jesus of Nazareth." He denied it again, with an oath: "I don't know the man!"** After a little while, those standing there went up to Peter and said, **"Surely you are one of them, for your accent gives you away." Then he began to call down curses on himself and he swore to them, "I don't know the man!"** Immediately a rooster crowed. Then Peter remembered the word Jesus had spoken: "Before the rooster crows, you will **disown me** three times." And he went outside and wept bitterly. (Mat 26:69-75)

Just like Peter, a real Christian can *disown* Jesus (or *fall away*). The Apostle Peter did this by denying he was with Jesus or knew Him. He didn't have to say, *I don't want you* (and it didn't have to be *lifestyle*). **What Peter said was enough to cause Jesus to disown Peter! If Jesus** *disowns* **you, then you can't be his sheep anymore, just like other unsaved people. Christians are described as God's possessions: his sheep (John 10:26,27; 21:16), his bride (Rev. 19:7), his body (Eph. 5:23; Col. 1:24); etc.**

Adam and Eve

The first act of disobedience by man in the Bible occurred in Gen. 3. God had forewarned Adam that the day he would eat from the tree of the knowledge of good and evil he would *die* (Gen. 2:17). That is exactly what happened **with a single act of sin.** It wasn't *lifestyle habitual practice*, but **a single act of sin that brought both Adam and Eve to their spiritual death.**

David Became An *Evildoer*

Shockingly, even people exceedingly strong in faith can afterwards stray to the point of committing sin that leads to death. David did this. David's glaring sins were one act of adultery and one act of murder, which would exclude him from God's kingdom and place him in the lake of fire (1 Cor. 6:9,10, Rev. 21:8). For at least 9 months, he was a bible-defined *adulterer* and *murderer* because of his single acts of adultery and murder. Nathan told David:

> Why did you despise the word of the LORD by **doing what is evil** in his eyes? You struck down Uriah the Hittite with the sword and took his wife to be your own. You killed him with the sword of the Ammonites. (2 Sam 12:9)

Note, David did what was *evil*. You might say this is no great revelation of truth. Of course adultery and murder are *evil*. But false teachers, some of whom say they reject eternal security, would declare David didn't lose his salvation, even though 1 Cor. 6:9,10 and Rev. 21:8 are so clear. When 2 Sam. 12:9 is coupled with this and the following, we have even more supportive evidence that David did lose his salvation at that dark time in his life:

David *Died* Spiritually

If I tell the righteous man that he will surely live, but then he trusts in his righteousness and **does evil**, none of the righteous things he has done will be remembered; **he will die for the evil he has done.** (Ezek 33:13)

Those who *do evil*, like David did, *die* spiritually, according to the above. The following is also evidence that David lost his salvation for a time:

But if a righteous man turns from his righteousness and commits sin and **does the same detestable things the wicked man does**, will he live? None of the righteous things he has done will be remembered. **Because of the unfaithfulness** he is guilty of **and because of the sins he has committed, he will die.** (Ezek 18:24)

If a righteous man **turns from his righteousness and does evil, he will die for it.** (Ezek 33:18)

If a righteous man **turns from his righteousness and commits sin, he will die for it; because of the sin he has committed he will die.** (Ezek 18:26)

Sadly, some will reject the clarity of these Scriptures and try to distort the facts to say that David didn't lose his salvation (*die*) after committing adultery and murder. **Such a person is as bad or even worse than an eternal security teacher, even though he might outwardly deny the teaching of eternal security.**

Note: The strong warnings of Ezek 18:24,26; 33:13,18 were not just *hypothetical*, as some say, **for such happened to David.**

Even David knew he was an *evil doer* during that time and hence **one who *died* spiritually (not physically) because of his sin:**

Have mercy on me, O God, according to your unfailing love; according to your great compassion blot out my transgressions. Wash away all my iniquity and cleanse me from my sin. For I know my transgressions, and my sin is always before me. Against you, you only, have I sinned and **done what is evil** in your sight, so that you are proved right when you speak and justified when you judge. (Psa 51:1-4)

Furthermore, some like to misuse Psa. 51 to say David only lost the joy of his salvation. They somehow miss how David humbly and sorrowfully asked God for **mercy** because of his sins, as just cited, which is also how Jesus said the repentant tax collector got saved (or *justified*):

But the tax collector stood at a distance. He would not even look up to heaven, but beat his breast and said, **"God, have mercy on me, a sinner."** I tell you that **this man**, rather than the other, **went home justified before God.** For everyone who exalts himself will be humbled, and he who **humbles himself** will be exalted. (Luke 18:13, 14)

After David prayed for mercy, forgiveness (and salvation), he also asked for other things like the joy of his salvation to be restored (Psa. 51:12). Psalm 51 is the prayer of a man who had backslidden to his own spiritual death.

Don't *Look Back* From The Plow

The Lord must have shocked the people of his day by teaching the following:

But Jesus said to him, "No one, after putting his hand to the plow and **looking back**, is fit for the kingdom of God." (Luke 9:62, NASB)

Another translation says:

Jesus replied, "No one who puts his hand to the plow and looks back is fit for service in the kingdom of God." (Luke 9:62, NIV)

There is no essential difference between these translations because those who do enter God's kingdom will *serve* Him there (Rev. 22:3). Not to be *fit for service* in the kingdom of God is not to enter the kingdom of

God, but to go to the lake of fire. Either way, **looking back will exclude one from the kingdom of God.**

God wants us to be faithful to him and love him more than any person or thing in this world. The Lord elevated this to **a salvation issue** (Mt. 10:37-39; Lk. 14:26,33). James commented similarly:

> You adulterous people, don't you know that friendship with the world is hatred toward God? **Anyone who chooses to be a friend of the world becomes an enemy of God.** (James 4:4)

Christian people who chose to be friends of the world become *enemies of God* again as they were before their salvation. That is the same as committing *spiritual adultery*. Remember also Lot's wife who looked back one time and was destroyed (Gen. 19:26). Jesus mentioned her:

> Remember Lot's wife. "Whoever seeks to keep his life **will lose it,** and whoever loses *his life* will preserve it." (Luke 17:32,33)

Your Words

People have a hard time believing that words can endanger a person to **hell fire,** but Jesus actually taught this:

> But I tell you that anyone who is angry with his brother will be subject to judgment. Again, anyone who says to his brother, "Raca," is answerable to the Sanhedrin. **But anyone who says, "You fool!" will be in danger of the fire of hell.** (Mat 5:22)

Through this single act, such extreme danger of *hell fire* becomes a reality, even for people previously saved. This parallels another eternal truth about words. Jesus also taught:

> But I tell you that men will have to give account on the day of judgment for **every careless word** they have spoken. For by your words you will be justified, and **by your words you will be condemned.** (Mat 12:37)

Your words can bring *condemnation* or the opposite which is *justification*. Remember, Peter *disowned* Jesus with his words.

Eternal Sin

It is also through words that a person can commit eternal sin, which will never be forgiven:

> But whoever blasphemes against the Holy Spirit will never be forgiven; he is guilty of an eternal sin. He said this because they were saying, "**He has an evil spirit.**" (Mark 3:29,30)

Notice please that eternal sin is committed through words. It also seems from this Scripture and the historical background of the book of Hebrews, that some of the people addressed there committed eternal sin and couldn't be renewed by repentance (Heb. 6:4-6). Raging fire was awaiting them, even though they had been previously sanctified by the blood of the covenant (Heb. 10:26-29). There was no eternal security for them and there is none for us today.

Idolaters

Paul wrote to those already saved and knew that their spiritual identity could be changed to *idolater* by a single act of this sin:

> **Do not be idolaters**, as some of them were; as it is written: "The people sat down to eat and drink and got up to indulge in pagan revelry." (1 Cor 10:7)

Paul referred to the golden calf incident in Exodus 32. Hence, by that **single act of idolatry they became *idolaters*** and he knew the same could happen to these Christians he addressed. Remember, *idolaters* will go to the lake of fire (Rev. 21:8).

The Mark of the Beast

In spite of the clear warning regarding the mark of the beast, many will take it because of the heavy pressure to do so. The saints who yield will lose their salvation with this single act of disobedience:

> A third angel followed them and said in a loud voice: "If **anyone** worships the beast and his image and receives his mark on the fore-

head or on the hand, he, too, will drink of the wine of God's fury, which has been poured full strength into the cup of his wrath. **He will be tormented with burning sulfur in the presence of the holy angels and of the Lamb.** And the smoke of their torment rises for ever and ever. **There is no rest day or night for those who worship the beast and his image, or for anyone who receives the mark of his name.**" This calls for patient endurance on the part of **the saints who** obey God's commandments and **remain faithful to Jesus.** (Rev 14:9-12)

Faithfulness to Jesus to the end of our life is needed for salvation, even though it might mean severe persecution and physical death:

Do not be afraid of what you are about to suffer. I tell you, the devil will put some of you in prison to test you, and you will suffer persecution for ten days. **Be faithful, even to the point of death**, and I will give you the crown of life. He who has an ear, let him hear what the Spirit says to the churches. **He who overcomes will not be hurt at all by the second death.** (Rev 2:10,11)

In Summary

There are various ways for a Christian to lose his salvation. Sometimes a single act of sin can do it, while at other times it won't happen as abruptly, as with being *lukewarm* (Rev. 3:15,16). Furthermore, one doesn't even have to sin to lose his salvation. He can lose it by believing a false gospel (1 Cor. 15:2 cf.1 John 2:24,25) or preaching a false gospel (Gal. 1:8,9). What a shock this is to those who have been deceived by those who change grace into a license for immorality by teaching David never lost his salvation or a single act of sin like adultery, suicide or drunkenness won't cause this. Jude identified all who change grace into a licence for immorality as ungodly (Jude 3,4), divisive, who don't have the Spirit (v. 19) and for whom blackest darkness is reserved forever (v. 13).

False teachers that declare *lifestyle sinning* not only ignore or twist the above Scriptures, but also dangerously portray the possibility of a loose, wild, immoral person as being a *Christian*. Ponder 1 Cor. 6:9,10 and the list there. (See also Eph. 5:5-7 and Rev. 21:8.) According to such false teachers, declaring their unscriptural version of *grace*, if a person previously saved commits occasional acts of **fornication, idolatry, adultery, being** effeminate, homosexuality, theft, covetousness, being drunk, reviling and swindling all at the same time he remains saved. This is a horrible and deadly distortion of the true *Christian* described in the Bible. Please note that Paul didn't have to consider the *lifestyle* of Elymas to know he was a *child of the devil* (Acts 13:10). See also 1 John 3:10.

Moreover, such a teacher proclaiming *lifestyle* sinning is no real friend of the immoral, since he is only endangering their souls to hell by misleading them with a false security and their so-called *grace* and *gospel* message. They are not being merciful or loving by preaching their lies and tickling the ears of the backslidden. The loving and vital message the immoral need to know is they must turn from such sin for salvation's sake.

False shepherds say the righteous person who becomes an *evil doer* can still go to heaven, but Jesus made it crystal clear such will instead rise to be *condemned* and thrown into *the fiery furnace:*

Those who have done good will rise to live, and **those who have done evil will rise to be condemned.** (John 5:29)

The Son of Man will send out his angels, and they will weed out of his kingdom **everything that causes sin** and **all who do evil.** They will **throw them into the fiery furnace**, where there will be weeping and gnashing of teeth. (Mat 13:41,42)

Both Are Just As *Deadly*

The bottom line difference between eternal security teachers, who unashamedly declare a Christian can commit the *occasional* acts of sin such as cited in 1 Cor. 6:9,10 and remain saved, and those who say they reject eternal security but teach the same, is non-existent! There really is no difference. Both are just as deadly and are misleading people to hell by their message. If you are a real Christian flee from such a congregation and so-called "pastor," regardless how convenient it may be to remain. Don't endanger your eternal soul and the souls of those you love by attending and supporting such a ravenous wolf in sheep's clothing. Don't share in his wicked work (2 John 10,11).

12

Eternal Security Is Another Gospel

How important is the teaching of eternal security to the eternal security teachers? In other words, is this topic of primary importance or merely a "non-essential"? The following quotes from the OSAS teachers will answer that question for us. This is what they have gone on record as saying regarding the importance of eternal security:

They Present it as the "Gospel":

> Eternal security is one of those outstanding glories of the Christian **gospel** (John Ankerberg).

> The very **gospel** itself comes under attack when the eternal security of the believer is questioned (Charles Stanley).

> One must believe in the perseverance of the saints if one is to accurately present **the gospel of grace**. To do anything else is to edit the **gospel** (James White).

> Calvinism is the **gospel** and nothing else (Charles Spurgeon).

They Present it as the "Atonement":

> The eternal security of the believer arises out of the necessity and nature of the **atonement** (Robert Morey).

They Present it as "Grace":

> What **grace** it is that can give us not only forgiveness and eternal life through faith alone but also guarantee that the Giver will never renege on His gift! Nor can we give it back even if we try! (Charles Ryrie).

> Once a son, always a son. Once you are born into the family of God, you will always be a member of the family of God. You cannot change your spiritual birth any more than you can change your physical birth ... the moment you believed in Jesus Christ as Lord and Savior, you were born into the family of God. At that point, you became a child of God, and for all eternity you will remain a child of God. **This is the grace of God**. There is nothing you can do to alter it (Robert Thieme, Jr.).

Calvinism is supposed to be "the doctrines of grace."

They Present it as "Foundational to Christianity":

> ... the very **foundations of Christianity** begin to crumble once we begin tampering with the eternal security of the believer (Charles Stanley).

They Have Taught "Heretics" Oppose the Perseverance of the Saints:

> The carnal mind is unable to comprehend this doctrine of the perseverance of the saints .... the **heretics** oppose it (Synod of Dort, Article 15).

Now that we know how this doctrine has been exalted to the zenith in importance by OSAS teachers themselves by equating it to **the gospel**, the **atonement, grace**, and **foundational to Christianity**, with **heretics** opposing it, let's now examine how they have presented their *gospel* to convince some people that it is Scriptural.

Eternal security teachers declare a partial truth about salvation as the whole truth and deceive their listeners by doing so. Five examples of this are:

1. They teach we are saved by grace not by works (Eph. 2:5-9), **but they stop there**! They never teach that Christians can *fall* from the *grace* that saves to the point where Christ is of *no value*:

    Mark my words! I, Paul, tell you that if you let yourselves be circumcised, **Christ will be of no value to you at all**. Again I declare to every man who lets himself be circumcised that he is obligated to obey the whole law. You who are trying to be justified by law have been alienated from Christ; **you have fallen away from grace.** (Gal 5:2-4)

    Comment: Since a Christian can *fall* from the grace by which he is saved, **then he would no longer be with the salvation he once had because of grace.** Furthermore, for a Christian to fall from grace to the point where Christ is of *no value at all*, can only mean **no more salvation!**

2. Eternal security teachers declare **we are justified by faith (Rom. 5:1), but they stop there**! They never proclaim the additional truth that a true believer can cease believing and *fall away* (or die spiritually):

    Those on the rock are the ones who receive the word with joy when they hear it, but they have no root. **They believe for a while**, but in the time of testing they **fall away**. (Lk 8:13)

    Comment: **A true believer can cease believing**, according to the Lord Jesus! Such would make him an *unbeliever*. Question: what did God Himself declare about the *unbelieving*? He taught:

    But the cowardly, the **unbelieving**, the vile, the murderers, the sexually immoral, those who practice magic arts, the idolaters and all liars—**their place will be in the fiery lake of burning sulfur.** This is the second death. (Rev 21:8)

Moreover, 1 Pet. 1:9 adds important truth to this by stating:

you are receiving the goal of your **faith**, the salvation of your souls.

Notice: The *goal* of our faith is *the salvation of our souls*. Hence, **if our faith gets destroyed, then there can be no salvation for our souls in the end.**

Finally, Paul believed a Christian could have his faith *shipwrecked* and told Timothy what he needed to do to prevent this from happening to him:

> holding on to faith and a good conscience. Some have rejected these and so have **shipwrecked their faith**. Among them are Hymenaeus and Alexander, whom I have handed over to Satan to be taught not to blaspheme. (1 Tim 1:19,20)

Note: Paul knew that Timothy's saving faith could become *shipwrecked*, as Hymenaeus and Alexander's faith did, and told him what to do to prevent this from happening to himself. The implications of that are: (a) A Christian has free will and human responsibilities under "grace" that can affect our salvation. (b) A Christian cannot just throw off all holy restraints and be negligent. For him to think that since he has been sealed by the Holy Spirit he is eternally secure or that God will continue to hold on to him, even if he lets go of God, is fallacious!

3.   OSAS teachers declare **eternal life is a "gift"** (Rom. 6:23) and **a present tense possession** (Jn. 6:47; 1 Jn. 5:12,13), **but they stop there**! The following supplementing Scriptures are not presented by them, which distorts the truth:

> That being justified by his grace, we should be made heirs according to the **hope** of eternal life. (Titus 3:7)

> The one who sows to please his sinful nature, from that nature will reap destruction; the one who sows to please the Spirit, from the Spirit **will reap eternal life**. Let us not become weary in doing good, for at the proper time we will reap a harvest **if we do not give up**. (Gal 6:8,9)

But he shall receive an hundredfold now in this time, houses, and brethren, and sisters, and mothers, and children, and lands, with persecutions; and **in the world to come eternal life.** (Mk 10:30)

To those who by persistence in doing good seek glory, honor and immortality, **he will give eternal life.** (Rom 2:7)

Jesus and His Apostles taught that eternal life is a *hope*, yet to be *reaped*, in *the world to come*, but only *if we do not give up* sowing to please the Spirit and *persist* in doing good!

Note: To get eternal life, **we must *persist* in doing good** (Rom. 2:7). This parallels how the Lord described those who would, in the end, enter the kingdom of God:

Those **who have done good** will rise to live, and those who have done evil will rise to be condemned. (Jn 5:29)

4.   Frequently, the OSASers will misuse Jude 24 by stating a partial truth about it as the whole truth:

Now unto him that is able to **keep** you from falling, and to present *you* faultless before the presence of his glory with exceeding joy (Jude 24).

They conclude that it is God who *keeps* us from *falling*. But they fail to mention that saved people still *fall* and even *fall away*! See Mt. 11:6; 26:31,33; Lk. 8:13; Heb. 6:6; 2 Pet. 1:10; 3:17; etc.

Under *grace* we are told as Christians to *keep* ourselves, according to the Lord Himself and His Apostles' teaching. The following verses are cited in their entirety so no one can falsely accuse me of *a works salvation* or *legalism*:

Be dressed ready for service and **keep** your lamps burning. (Lk 12:35)

The man who loves his life will lose it, while the man who hates his life in this world will **keep** it for eternal life. (Jn 12:25)

Religion that God our Father accepts as pure and faultless is this: to look after orphans and widows in their distress and to **keep** oneself from being polluted by the world. (Jam 1:27)

Keep yourselves in God's love as you wait for the mercy of our Lord Jesus Christ to bring you to eternal life. (Jude 21)

Dear children, **keep** yourselves from idols. (1 Jn 5:21)

... do not share in the sins of others. **Keep** yourself pure. (1 Tim 5:22)

5. Eternal security teachers oftentimes refer to certain religious people as *never really being saved to begin with,* based on Mt. 7:23:

Then I will tell them plainly, "I never knew you. Away from me, you evildoers!"

But additional truth from Mt. 25:1-12 reveals that five out of ten virgins from the last generation will have their lamps stop burning before the Lord returns. They will hear the Lord say something different to them:

I tell you the truth, **I don't know you.** (Mt 25:12)

Comment: The Lord Jesus did not say to those five foolish virgins, "I *never* knew you," but instead stated that He did not know those virgins any longer, with the words, *I don't know you.*

As just proven, eternal security teachers declare a partial truth about salvation as the whole truth and deceive their listeners by doing so. Related facts are not mentioned, but rather avoided, which changes the conclusion from OSAS to a conditional security. Friend, remember the following:

■ A Christian can fall from *grace* to the point where Christ is of *no value* to him.
■ A saving faith in Christ can become *shipwrecked.* Also a true believer can cease believing and become an unbeliever.
■ Eternal life is a *hope,* yet to be *reaped, in the age to come,* but only for the ones who *sow to please the Spirit, persist in doing good* and *don't give up.*

- Under *grace*, Christians are commanded to *keep* themselves.
- A person once *known* by God can later become unknown!

Besides partial truths presented as the whole truth, eternal security is also built on Scriptures used out of context! This too has deceived their listeners. For example, the wonderful promise of John 10:28,29 can only be properly understood in its context, which goes back to v. 27:

> My sheep hear my voice, and I know them, and **they follow me**: And I give unto them eternal life; and **they shall never perish, neither shall any *man* pluck them out of my hand.** My Father, which gave *them* me, is greater than all; and **no *man* is able to pluck *them* out of my Father's hand.** (Jn 10:27-29)

Some people see salvation with "no strings attached," that is, regardless how far one may stray doctrinally or sinfully, he will always be of the group that shall *never perish*. But the context of Jn. 10:27-29 destroys this deadly interpretation of the most commonly cited proof text for eternal security. Verse 27 describes the sheep and states they *follow* Jesus. The Greek word is a **continuous tense** and describes the only people that will *never perish* and won't get *plucked* out of God's hand (vv. 28,29).

Hence: OSAS is a false gospel and counterfeit grace message built upon partial truths presented as the whole truth and distorted Scriptures, as just proven.

More truth on the subject of salvation reveals that the Bible teaches a conditional security for the believer. For example, the Lord Jesus taught those already saved:

> And ye shall be hated of all *men* for my name's sake: but **he that endureth to the end shall be saved.** (Mt 10:22)

Note: Jesus spoke those words to His disciples as they were being sent out to preach and heal. The context is **not** the Jews during the tribulation period, as eternal security teachers usually say! Moreover, Jesus was **not** joking when He taught Christians they would have to endure **to the end for salvation's sake!**

Furthermore, the Lord taught Christians, after his infinite work on the cross:

Do not be afraid of what you are about to suffer. I tell you, the devil will put some of you in prison to test you, and you will suffer persecution for ten days. **Be faithful, even to the point of death**, and I will give you the crown of life. He who has an ear, let him hear what the Spirit says to the churches. He who overcomes will not be hurt at all by **the second death**. (Rev 2:10,11)

Comment: Jesus mentioned faithfulness, but **not** God's faithfulness to us as stressed by the OSAS teachers, but **our faithfulness to God** *even to the point of death*. Such a person is promised something to receive and not receive. He will receive the crown of life and won't be hurt by the "second death" (another name for *the lake of fire*, according to Rev. 21:8).

The Writer of Hebrews Concisely Declared:

We have come to share in Christ **if we hold firmly till the end the confidence we had at first.** (Heb 3:14)

Paul, the real grace teacher, also wrote:

By this gospel you are saved, **if you hold firmly** to the word I preached to you. **Otherwise, you have believed in vain.** (1 Cor 15:2)

But now he has reconciled you by Christ's physical body through death to present you holy in his sight, without blemish and free from accusation—**if you continue in your faith**, established and firm, not moved from the hope held out in the gospel. This is the gospel that you heard and that has been proclaimed to every creature under heaven, and of which I, Paul, have become a servant. (Col 1:22,23)

1 Cor. 15:2 and Col. 1:22,23 declare the true gospel of grace has a **conditional security for the believer** attached to it! That was the original message, as taught by the Lord Himself and His Apostles. **Do not be deceived by the OSAS false gospel and counterfeit grace message, which is built upon partial truths and Scripture removed from its context.**

All documentation for this chapter can be found in our book, *The Believer's Conditional Security.*

13

Eternal Security And The Sin Unto Death

You will probably never hear any eternal security teacher say outrightly their doctrine is a *license for immorality*. In fact, they will most often flatly deny this charge sometimes to the point of yelling *slander*. However, there are still various ways these people teach this very thing they hate to be identified with. Certainly one is through their version of the *sin unto death*. The apostle John wrote of this sin:

> If anyone sees his brother commit a sin that does not lead to death, he should pray and God will give him life. I refer to those whose sin does not lead to death. There is **a sin that leads to death**. I am not saying that he should pray about that. All wrongdoing is sin, and there is sin that does not lead to death. (1 John 5:16,17)

Clearly, there is sin that leads to death. Whatever type of *death* this is, is not clearly identified here. However, the eternal security teachers like to draw our attention to 1 Cor. 11:27-30, which reads:

> Therefore, whoever eats the bread or drinks the cup of the Lord in an unworthy manner will be guilty of sinning against the body and blood of the Lord. A man ought to examine himself before he eats of the bread and drinks of the cup. For anyone who eats and drinks without recognizing the body of the Lord eats and drinks **judgment on himself**. That is why many among you are weak and sick, and **a number of you have fallen asleep.**

And to that they sometimes add the deaths of Ananias and Sapphira as specific examples of the sin unto death:

> Then Peter said, "Ananias, how is it that Satan has so filled your heart that you have **lied to the Holy Spirit** and have kept for yourself some of the money you received for the land? Didn't it belong to you before it was sold? And after it was sold, wasn't the money at your disposal? What made you think of doing such a thing? You have not lied to men but to God." **When Ananias heard this, he fell down and died**. And great fear seized all who heard what had happened. Then the young men came forward, wrapped up his body, and carried him out and buried him. About three hours later his wife came in, not knowing what had happened. Peter asked her, "Tell me, is this the price you and Ananias got for the land?" "Yes," she said, "that is the price." Peter said to her, "How could you agree to test the Spirit of the Lord? Look! The feet of the men who buried your husband are at the door, and they will carry you out also." At that moment **she fell down at his feet and died**. Then the young men came in and, finding her dead, carried her out and buried her beside her husband. (Acts 5:3-10)

To Them *Death* Is Always Physical

To the eternal security teachers *death* will always be physical death, such as mentioned in 1 Cor. 11:30 and Acts 5:3-10. **While it is undeniable truth that God gets so angry over sin that he kills people because of it,** there is another truth related to this that the eternal security teachers will always deny—that **sin can bring a Christian to his spiritual death, just like Adam and Eve *died spiritually* because of their sin**, as God warned would happen (Gen. 2:17). (God didn't kill them physically but they did *die* spiritually like he warned.)

From the eternal security perspective, when a person who was formerly saved would die physically, he will **always** go to heaven. How such people are living at that point is inconsequential, **even if God would kill them physically because of their unrepentant *heinous* sins. This clearly spells out *license for immorality*.**

Dave Hunt's *License For Immorality*

Please note what Dave Hunt teaches about this as he comments on the 1 Cor. 11 passage:

For this cause, some of you are weak and sickly and some of you sleep; some of you died because **God has brought judgment upon you for the way you have conducted yourselves and so forth**. So I think what he's saying is, there are **some sins that are so heinous** and **not only heinous** but perhaps I think it depends upon the position that a person has that **brings reproach upon Christ and God takes them home** for that.[1]

Judgment or Blessing?

To be consistent with his *license for immorality* or his *security-in-sin gospel*, commonly called eternal security (once saved always saved, the perseverance of the saints or the preservation of the saints), Dave Hunt must always teach the way just cited. Question for Dave Hunt (and all other eternal security people): What kind of punishment is this that God would kill people because of their unrepentant heinous sins and take them out of this cursed environment filled with sin, injustice and pain to a beautiful paradise where joy, peace, truth, righteousness, etc. will be? For Paul, to live was Christ and die was *gain* and *better by far* (Phil. 1:21-23), but these "blind guides" want us to think we can live for self, sin and the devil and die in those sins and that death is *gain* when God kills you in his anger. **Hence, death isn't really a punishment at all, but a *blessing* and *gain* for their hatred of God.**

To look at this in another way, one can therefore backslide into *heinous* sin and wickedness, absolutely refuse to repent even though disciplined and be blessed by the thrice holy God for their unyielding stubborn rebellion when he strikes them dead in his holy wrath and anger. Dear reader, if you ponder the horrible conclusion produced by the eternal security teachers, you will have to agree that this is nothing

---

1   Radio show 0121. (The word, heinous, is defined as "utterly reprehensible or evil.")

more than a deadly, religious myth yielding an opportunity and license to live in *wild* rebellion to God—*a license for immorality.*

Hunt And The Calvinists—Close Associates

The so-called *Berean* Dave Hunt is not alone with these Scriptural fabrications and distortions. **Hunt has the staunch Calvinists as his close companions and co-laborers with this teaching, even though he claims to oppose Calvinism!** Please note what Calvinist D. James Kennedy has likewise written about this:

> I think back many years ago of **a man in this church who was engaged in adultery**—a man who had been a minster [sic] and had left the ministry, but a man who seemed to be a godly man—a man who seemed to be a Christian. Only God knows the heart. He **became involved with a married woman**. He was going to have her divorce her husband and marry him. I admonished him and urged him to repent. He was brought before the discipline committee and they admonished him to repent. He was suspended from the sacraments, but **he did not repent.** Finally, the Session determined that since **he remained impenitent,** they would have to excommunicate this man from the church. Just before that happened, God pulled his string and **suddenly that young man died.**
>
> These are just some of the unlimited, infinite ways God can chasten **those who are truly His own**, who do not repent of their sins. My friends, we need to take the warnings seriously because they are very real.[2]

So Hunt and the Calvinists are identical twins regarding the sin unto death, because they both teach eternal security, that is, once a person becomes saved he will always remain saved regardless how far into wickedness he may go and remain.

---

2   D. James Kennedy, *Can A Christian Fall From Grace?* (Ft. Lauderdale FL: Coral Ridge Ministries), pp. 14, 15.

Calvinism's Christian *Adulterers*

Kennedy's message comes through loud and clear regarding his so-called *doctrines of grace*. **He is indirectly saying by his story that Christian adulterers do exist**. In contrast to this deadly doctrinal myth, the Bible speaks of only one type of adulterer and he is always shown as one who will not inherit the kingdom of God (1 Cor. 6:9,10), but instead will be thrown into the lake of fire (Rev. 21:8), unless he repents. **But the eternal security teachers don't think this person has to repent for salvation. He will still get to heaven and escape hell in his unrepentant** *adultery* **or** *heinous* **sins, because he was once saved!** How God must hate this deadly lie which has multitudes deceived.

At times Kennedy's Calvinism will have him declare **the elect will endure in holiness to the end**, but then he turns right around and blatantly teaches his *sin unto death* yarn. Doesn't Kennedy know that dying in adultery is not *enduring to the end in holiness?*

God Lovers and God Haters

Dear eternal security reader, you have been deceived by popular teachers of our hour and from yesteryear that have changed grace into *a license for immorality,* as just proven. This should be apparent now after considering what both types of eternal security teachers have said about *the sin unto death.* **Their deadly version of grace allows or permits all forms of unrepentant wickedness for those that enter heaven**. In contrast, the Bible says the following:

However, as it is written: "No eye has seen, no ear has heard, no mind has conceived what God has prepared **for those who love him."** (1 Cor 2:9)

Listen, my dear brothers: Has not God chosen those who are poor in the eyes of the world to be rich in faith and to **inherit the kingdom he promised those who love him**? (James 2:5)

In other words, **those who actually enter God's kingdom** *love* **God.** (This is the real issue, not if God loves them.) **To love God we must** *obey* **him** (John 14:15,21,23,24; 1 John 5:3). Moreover, not to love Jesus is to be unsaved:

> If anyone does not love the Lord, **he is to be accursed**. Maranatha. (1 Cor 16:22)

Clearly, one is not *loving* God if he is in such sins as those just taught by the well-known Hunt and Kennedy. Jesus taught:

> **He who does not love me will not obey my teaching**.... (John 14:24)

God promises to kill those who *hate* him—his adversaries:

> See now that I myself am He! There is no god besides me. **I put to death** and I bring to life, I have wounded and I will heal, and no one can deliver out of my hand. I lift my hand to heaven and declare: As surely as I live forever, **when I sharpen my flashing sword and my hand grasps it in judgment, I will take vengeance on my adversaries and repay those who hate me.** (Deut 32:39-41)

Furthermore, Hebrews 10:26,27 say:

> For if we go on sinning willfully after receiving the knowledge of the truth, there no longer remains a sacrifice for sins, but a terrifying expectation of judgment and **the fury of a fire which will consume the adversaries.**

Did you notice that one becomes an enemy of God by turning to willful sin (or deliberate sin), the very thing Hunt and Kennedy teachings allow for without jeopardizing one's salvation. Also, Heb. 10:27 says *the fury of fire* (or raging fire) will consume God's adversaries. How much more clear can it get? **Nowhere does the Bible say that God in His wrath kills those in unrepentant, habitual sin and sends them to Heaven.**

Also, the true Christian is clearly called by the term *saint,* which means *holy one*. **Since sin can make a holy person unholy again** (1 Tim. 5:22; Rev. 3:4; etc.), and therefore unfit for entrance into the kingdom of God (Mt. 5:8; Heb. 12:14; Rom. 6:22; etc.), then **these eternal security teachers are dangerously downplaying the effects of sin in the life of a Christian. Souls are at risk because of their fables.**

The Real Truth

The real truth is a true Christian can sin in such a way as to bring him back into spiritual death and endanger him to the lake of fire again (James 1:14-16; 5:19,20; Luke 15:24,32; Gal. 5:19-21; 6:8,9; Rom. 6:16; 8:13; Rev. 2:10,11; etc.). **This is the real *sin unto death*, as mentioned by the Apostle John.** Moreover, if God in his holy wrath strikes someone dead because of his unrepentant adultery **he will go to hell**, not heaven, with other God haters as already shown in Hebrews. This was basic knowledge in first century Christianity, though popularly denied in our dark day by those who maintain their security-in-sin gospel and *license for immorality.*

Repent For Your Salvation's Sake

Dear reader, if you think you can live in *heinous* sin, as Hunt and Kennedy want all to believe, and still be on the road to heaven, you have been dangerously deceived. You must repent (turn from sin) or you will find yourself being thrown into the lake of fire in the end. You are not just jeopardizing your physical life, rewards, etc. as they say, but **it is your very soul that is endangered**. Don't be deceived.

Dear children, **do not let anyone lead you astray. He who does what is right is righteous, just as he is righteous. He who does what is sinful is of the devil....** (1 John 3:7,8)

14 _____

Nine Reasons Why I Hate Eternal Security

Recently, I was asked on a radio show what compels me to oppose the teaching of eternal security as I do. My answer, in part, was *I hate the teaching of eternal security*. No doubt some people will think this language is just too strong for a Christian to use, especially in these days of compromise and ecumenical unity. However, my answer was very Biblical:

A righteous man **hates** falsehood .... (Prov 13:5)

I **hate** and despise falsehood, *But* I love Your law. (Psa 119:163)

Hate evil, you who love the LORD ... (Psa 97:10)

The fear of the LORD is to **hate** evil ... (Prov 8:13)

... **Abhor** what is evil .... (Rom 12:9)

Moreover, in this chapter you will read some terms that might sound harsh as they describe those who are supposed to be representing God's precious truths, but are instead teaching dangerous lies. **All these terms are found in the Scriptures and they too are Biblical.**

Since many who will read this chapter have not come to the place where they know **eternal security is not a Christian teaching**, they will have trouble relating this popular teaching to something that is untruthful and hazardous, but it is every bit these and even more. This deadly lie has served the devil well since the first time he used it at Gen. 3:4 to bring about the spiritual death of Eve (and Adam afterwards) and has been implementing it ever since, especially since the days of John Calvin until now.

Reason #1

Because of the teaching of eternal security wickedness has flourished throughout the so-called "Christian" church on a global scale. There is no way for any man to calculate the broken homes through divorce, suicides and criminal acts that have been committed because people have been deceived into thinking their salvation is secure regardless what they do or fail to do. So-called Christian counselors and "Bible Answer" men have openly told suicidal people over the air that if they were ever saved and later decided to murder themselves, they will surely go to heaven. We have on audio tape a suicidal woman who called into the *Bible Answer Man* show and said, *If I knew I was going to heaven I would do it* [commit suicide], **but on the other hand** *I wouldn't want to do it if I was going to hell.* **That woman has set the precedent regarding eternal security leading to suicide, since she was both suicidal and an eternal security proponent. (By the way, the two eternal security teachers who told her she'd go to heaven were Paul Carden and Ron Rhodes.)**

Furthermore, eternal security is taught to prisoners. Since we receive letters directly from prisoners, we know from what they have written that even they are not safe from these deadly lies and distortions that will foster more crime for some after they are freed. For some people so caught up in sin and wickedness, they have to spend time in jail to ponder life and values. Prison is a golden opportunity for some to repent and find salvation. But in that broken humbled state the devil still sends his message of eternal security to even them, as we have learned.

Perhaps the home has been hurt more by eternal security than any other heresy in our adulterous day. **We have an audio excerpt where the so-called** *pastor* **Donald Cole tells a married woman whose husband left her and moved in with another woman, that if he (the adulterer), was ever saved he** *is on the road to heaven and will never get off the road to heaven.* **Only God knows how many people that heard this wicked lie had the first thoughts of being unfaithful to their spouse, since they too** *will never get off the road to heaven.* But that is only one of hundreds of times such a deadly distortion has been stated over radio by these blind leaders.

Besides all of that we have the personal testimony of **a man who started to drink alcohol and became an alcoholic for 16 years because a loved one told him about** *once saved always saved* at a time when he was spiritually weak, weary and persecuted. He accepted the idea that living godly was *optional* and not necessary for salvation. This snowballed into more sin, until he finally repented and became *alive again*, like the prodigal (Lk 15:24).

Reason #2

The teachers of eternal security are masters of deception. How they avoid such a large body of Scriptures and distort others to present this doctrine is truly an infernal talent. To distort any teaching (especially something related to salvation itself) such as the believer's security is most serious, but how much more when these grace changers connect eternal security with the *gospel* **itself. Charles Stanley, the most dangerous eternal security teacher alive, has boldly done this very thing. Imagine teaching a** *heresy* **as the** *gospel* **itself. This is, in fact, what is being done at this present time. Woe to Stanley and all others who preach their security-in-sin** *gospel*:

> But even if we, or an angel from heaven, should preach to you a gospel contrary to what we have preached to you, **he is to be accursed!** As we have said before, so I say again now, **if any man is preaching to you a gospel contrary to what you received, he is to be accursed!** (Gal 1:8,9)

So what is the real *gospel* that Paul preached and first-century Christians of the Bible believed? It is found in a Scripture that the eternal security teachers like to skip over when citing the gospel from 1 Cor. 15:

> By this gospel you are saved, **if you hold firmly** to the word I preached to you. **Otherwise, you have believed in vain.** (1 Cor 15:2)

Clearly, the real gospel has a conditional security written all over it, in contrast to what the savage wolves in sheep's clothing want us all to believe.

Reason #3

The greatest example that Christianity has ever produced was the Apostle Paul. This man shed his blood on at least nine different occasions, spent years in prison, often suffered from lack and frequently risked his health and life to be faithful to his precious Lord. However, the teachers who change *grace into a license for immorality* (Jude 3,4) would like us all to believe that after becoming a Christian he was the chief of *sinners*, by not being able to live up to the very things he taught other Christians to do! How they impugn the holy character of Paul alone is enough to make me *hate* this lie that has certainly sent multitudes to hell over the years. How quick the deceivers are to say Paul declared *O wretched man that I am* trying to connect that statement to sin, but somehow overlooking (or ignoring) the following verses describing him:

> You are witnesses, and so is God, of how **holy, righteous and blameless** we were among you who believed. (1 Th 2:10)

> For this reason I am sending to you Timothy, my son whom I love, who is faithful in the Lord. He will remind you of **my way of life in Christ Jesus, which agrees with what I teach everywhere in every church.** (1 Cor 4:17)

> Whatever you have learned or received or heard from me, or **seen in me—put it into practice.** And the God of peace will be with you. (Phil 4:9)

> Now this is our boast: Our conscience testifies that **we have conducted ourselves in the world,** and especially in our relations with you, **in the holiness and sincerity that are from God.** We have done so not according to worldly wisdom but **according to God's grace.** (2 Cor 1:12)

After the Lord Jesus, Paul was the prize example of godliness and commitment we have in Scripture. But in their misplaced zeal for the doctrine of eternal security, these deceivers smear Paul's holy image as well as being a true Christian and try to replace it with permission for wickedness, worldliness and fruitlessness among the saints. The eternal security fleecers have no qualms to overlook the above Scriptures and many others like them. They teach there are two types of adulterers, two types of drunkards, two types of murderers, etc.—one being unsaved because he never had a moment of faith and the other being saved because he did, **even though both have identical behavior.** If they ever presented Paul as the Bible declares him to be, that would make it too hard for their security-in-sin myth to prevail, since they declare no one can live above sin and we all must sin all the time. **Woe to the eternal security teachers.**

Reason #4

These eternal security teachers often talk in a way that makes the unwary think they are exalting the infinite, finished work of Christ and His precious cleansing blood, but in reality they are actually downplaying these. This is especially apparent if one would read what they say about 2 Peter 2:20-22:

> If they have **escaped the corruption of the world by knowing our Lord and Savior Jesus Christ and are again entangled in it and overcome**, they are worse off at the end than they were at the beginning. It would have been better for them not to have known the way of righteousness, than to have known it and then to turn their backs on the sacred command that was passed on to them. Of them the proverbs are true: "A dog returns to its vomit," and, "A sow that is washed goes back to her wallowing in the mud."

To protect their doctrine they must sometimes deal with these "problem" passages, as they might call them, which *only seem* to teach contrary to their unconditional security. I have read on more than one occasion how they endeavor to explain away what Peter wrote about **those that return to their sins after *escaping* their entanglement in them.** Perhaps in their ignorance they are unaware they are actually demeaning the blood of Jesus by their interpretation. The truth is: **it is only coming into contact with the blood of Christ at the point of salvation that will enable one to be freed from sin's slavery and bondage which the people in 2 Peter 2:20,21 did experience.** Nothing else according to Scripture will do this; and the eternal security teachers have never produced a Scripture to show something else can. However, their wordy explanations are presented and ears that want to be tickled quickly nod in agreement when they try to explain why the people of 2 Peter 2:20-22 were *never really saved*, and thus protect their doctrine once again.

Reason #5

How distressing to hear the eternal security teachers imply, under their understanding of the faithfulness of God, that *Jesus is a liar* by blatantly contradicting him. The Lord taught the following as did Paul (who was merely repeating the Lord's teaching):

> But **whoever disowns me before men, I will disown him before my Father** in heaven. (Mt. 10:33)

> If we endure, we will also reign with him. **If we disown him, he will also disown us**. (2 Tim 2:12)

The eternal security teachers contradict these by drawing one's attention to 2 Tim. 2:13:

> **if we are faithless, he will remain faithful, for he cannot disown himself.**

But as they often do, they have lifted that verse away from its context and applied an interpretation which negates the verse before, as well as Mt. 10:33. Here's the context of that Scripture:

> Here is a trustworthy saying: If we died with him, we will also live with him; if we endure, we will also reign with him. **If we disown him, he will also disown us**; if we are faithless, he will remain faithful, for he cannot disown himself. (2 Tim 2:11-13)

The proper understanding of 2 Tim. 2:11-13 is if a Christian would disown (or deny) Jesus (as Peter did three times) and thereby show he is faithless at that point, God will remain faithful and disown (or deny) us, as Paul just wrote, which was a repeat of Jesus' teaching in Mt. 10:33. If God did not disown such a person, he would be disowning himself by going against his word. **Hence, by allowing for Christians to disown Christ without endangering their salvation, the eternal security blind guides have indirectly called Jesus a *liar* by blatantly contradicting his teach-**

ing found in Mt. 10:33, with their twisted interpretations. (Chuck Swindoll has taught we can deny him, but he won't deny us—the exact opposite of the Christian message.)

Reason #6

Besides everything else the teaching of eternal security does, it even goes further and attempts to *mock* God. Carefully read what Paul, the real *grace* teacher, revealed during his ministry about this:

> Do not be deceived: **God cannot be mocked. A man reaps what he sows.** The one who sows to please his sinful nature, from that nature will **reap destruction**; the one who sows to please the Spirit, from the Spirit will **reap eternal life**. Let us not become weary in doing good, for at the proper time we will reap a harvest if we do not give up. (Gal. 6:7-9)

People who know not what they are doing, attempt to *mock* God by teaching, in essence, you can reap eternal life even though you sow to please the *sinful nature* (or *flesh*). This, in truth, is the very heart of the security-in-sin gospel. But Paul said, *Do not be deceived.* It will not happen. Instead *you will reap what you sow.* If you sow to please your sinful nature, you will reap *destruction* instead of *eternal life*. To reap eternal life, you must sow to please the Spirit. (NOTE: This is not a *rewards* passage as the eternal security deceivers try to change it into. This is a *salvation* passage for it tells about reaping *eternal life*.)

Reason #7

There is still more just cause to *hate* eternal security, since a whole book of the Bible has been written about these teachers and their changing *grace* into a license for immorality. The book of Jude is not written for Christians to *contend* against those who attack the deity of Christ or his bodily resurrection or his return to earth, etc. It was specifically written about and against those who change *grace* into something it is not—*a license for immorality*:

> Dear friends, although I was very eager to write to you about the salvation we share, I felt I had to write and urge you to contend for the

faith that was once for all entrusted to the saints. For certain men whose **condemnation** was written about long ago have secretly slipped in among you. They are **godless men, who change the grace of our God into a license for immorality** and deny Jesus Christ our only Sovereign and Lord. (Jude 3,4)

While many in our dark day can see the real reason Jude told all Christians to contend against such false teachers, many of these same people refuse to identify the grace changers as Jude labeled them—*godless* (v.4), who *have rushed for profit into Balaam's error* (v.11), *shepherds who feed only themselves* (v. 12), for whom *blackest darkness has been reserved* (v. 13) and they *do not have the Spirit* (19). Please read through Jude carefully for yourself and you will be surprised how Jude describes the popular eternal security teachers of our day that have influence over millions of people because of their books, TV and/or radio ministries.

 Seeing the eternal security teachers, as God sees them, also shows how serious it is to support their local congregations and ministries or even just *tolerate* them:

If anyone comes to you and does not bring this teaching, do not take him into your house or welcome him. Anyone who welcomes him **shares in his wicked work.** (2 John 10,11)

Nevertheless, I have this against you: You **tolerate that woman Jezebel**, who calls herself a prophetess. **By her teaching she misleads my servants into sexual immorality** and the eating of food sacrificed to idols. (Rev 2:20)

You will share in the wicked work (or righteous work) of the people you support and help provide a platform for, according to Scripture. **How then can those of you who know eternal security is not a Christian teaching continue to support such a deadly, Christ-dishonoring doctrine taught by *godless* people? How can you *tolerate* these teachers who are misleading others into sexual immorality and other forms of wickedness?**

 The reader should know that a pastor, counter-cult ministry, apologist, evangelist, missionary, seminary professor, etc. **that teaches eternal security will be teaching unscripturally in many others areas too. It is not just the one area of eternal security that is dangerously wrong!**

Instead, hundreds of Scriptures will be distorted, shaded and slanted towards this doctrine or explained away in some fashion which produces some very strange and weird teachings leading one further from Biblical truth and into error.

Reason #8

The importance of *holiness* is shown in the following Scripture:

> But now that you have been set free from sin and have become slaves to God, the benefit you reap leads to **holiness**, and the result is **eternal life**. (Rom 6:22)

Though this Scripture is seldom quoted and hardly known, it is clearly a salvation passage, as evident by the words *eternal life*. Two other Scriptures that tie *holiness* and *heart purity* to an entrance into God's kingdom are:

> Make every effort to live in peace with all men and to be holy; **without holiness no one will see the Lord**. (Heb 12:14)

> **Blessed are the pure in heart, for they will see God**. (Mt 5:8)

At the point of salvation, one is washed by Jesus' blood and made perfectly clean and pure (Acts 15:9), but after this point, sin can bring defilement, contamination and even spiritual death:

> Remember, therefore, what you have received and heard; obey it, and repent. But if you do not wake up, I will come like a thief, and you will not know at what time I will come to you. **Yet you have a few people in Sardis who have not soiled their clothes. They will walk with me, dressed in white, for they are worthy**. (Rev 3:3,4)

> And He was saying, "That which proceeds out of the man, that is what defiles the man. For from within, out of the heart of men, proceed the evil thoughts, fornications, thefts, murders, adulteries, deeds of coveting *and* wickedness, *as well as* deceit, sensuality, envy, slander, pride *and* foolishness. All these evil things proceed from within and **defile the man**." (Mark 7:20-23)

For if you live according to the sinful nature, **you will die**; but if by the Spirit you put to death the misdeeds of the body, you will live, (Rom 8:13)

These are just a few of the many Scriptures that prove this point. In light of all this data, **eternal security is clearly an attack on *holiness*. In fact, eternal security is the greatest doctrinal threat to Biblical *holiness* that exists.**

Reason #9

The doctrine of eternal security also permits one, after the point of getting born again, to just *sit back, relax* and do *nothing* and still enter heaven after death, that is, if you believe this doctrinal myth. Both Charles Stanley and J. Vernon McGee have taught this (as well as multitudes of others). In contrast, God's word declares:

Every tree that does not bear good fruit is cut down and thrown into the fire. (Mt 7:19)

Someone asked him, "Lord, are only a few people going to be saved?" He said to them, "Make every effort to enter through the narrow door, because many, I tell you, will try to enter and will not be able to." (Lk 13:23,24)

... do not share in the sins of others. Keep yourself pure. (1 Tim 5:22)

Dear children, keep yourselves from idols. (1 John 5:21)

Then the man who had received the one talent came. "Master," he said, "I knew that you are a hard man, harvesting where you have not sown and gathering where you have not scattered seed. So I was afraid and went out and hid your talent in the ground. See, here is what belongs to you." His master replied, "You wicked, lazy servant! So you knew that I harvest where I have not sown and gather where I have not scattered seed? Well then, you should have put my money on deposit with the bankers, so that when I returned I would have received it back with interest. **Take the talent from him and give it to the one who has the ten talents**. For everyone who has will be given more, and he will have an abundance. Whoever does not have, even what he has will be taken from him. **And throw that worthless servant outside, into the darkness, where there will be weeping and gnashing of teeth.**" (Mt. 25:24-30)

The original message to the disciples was always *remain true to the Lord with all* your *[their] hearts* (Acts 11:23); *remain true to the faith* (Acts 14:22); etc. The responsibility for this was upon them as they got spiritual power from God. It is highly possible a Christian can fall away, get a shipwrecked faith, fall from grace, believe in vain, etc. Early Christians were told what to do and what not to do, what to say and what not to say, what to think about and what not to think about, how to dress and how not to dress. But all this is swept away under today's perverted version of *grace* as *legalism* or a *works salvation* and people who have experienced salvation consequently *relax*, as they have been taught by savage wolves in sheep's clothing and shown by example. **It seems the eternal security teachers will read hundreds of pages of the Bible to find anything they can use that seems to allow for slothfulness, wickedness and the like in the life of a Christian.**

Furthermore, lukewarmness can lead to a spiritual discharge from the Body of Christ. The Lord wants us [boiling] *hot* not lukewarm (Rev. 3:15, 16). But why should we even try if we will always remain saved regardless what we do or fail to do? Hence, the deceived think they can just blend in with the godless world system, which will prevent persecution problems. *I'll always remain saved*, these people think. But the Biblical record says *keep making every effort to enter the narrow* **[kingdom]** *doors* (Lk. 13:24), *keep your lamps burning* (Lk. 12:35), work in the vineyard (Mt. 21:28), *occupy* [keep busy] till Jesus returns (Lk. 19:13, KJV), put your hand to the plow (Lk. 9:62), abound in the work of the Lord (1 Cor. 15:58), etc. Moreover, the message of the Holy Spirit to Christians remains the same: be zealous always and *work* with all your heart as unto the Lord (Rom. 12:11; Col. 3:23).

In Summary

Eternal security, which began with the devil himself in Eden: (1) is responsible for **broken homes through divorce, suicides, alcoholism, porn addiction, criminal acts and much more** as it has deceived multitudes into thinking they are on the road to heaven when they are really on the road to hell; (2) **contradicts the real** *gospel* with a false security-in-sin gospel; (3) **slanders the Apostle Paul** in an attempt to allow for wickedness, worldliness and fruitlessness among Christians; (4) **downplays the precious blood of Christ** which alone can set one free from sin's slavery; (5) **indirectly calls Jesus a** *liar*; (6) **attempts to** *mock* **God**; (7) **has a book of the New Testament written warning about it and its teachers**; (8) is **the greatest doctrinal threat to** *holiness* as it downplays the seriousness of sin in the life of a Christian; and (9) **breeds lukewarmness while the Christian is taken off his spiritual guard to just** *relax*, instead of being diligent to bear good fruit, as we must do to avoid being thrown into the fire.

Eternal security needs to be exposed and refuted as never before. May Almighty God raise up many for this very purpose and may He also close down *every* **mission, ministry, congregation, seminary, etc. that spreads this sinister doctrine as well as drying up all funds used to support it.**

The message of enduring to the end *to be saved* **(Mt. 10:22) is the other part of the salvation message that is not being preached in our day, but instead has been attacked and rejected by people calling themselves** *Christians*. **A person needs to get saved and stay saved, which doesn't always happen.**

15 _____

The Accusation Of
A Works Salvation

One of the chief accusations cited by those who embrace *once saved always saved* (also known as *eternal security* or *the perseverance of the saints*), is that their opposition **is teaching a *works salvation***. In fact, it has been taught or suggested that one either believes in once saved always saved (OSAS) or ***must*** believe in a *works salvation*. Here are two actual emails we received which show this:

> If you believe that once saved always saved is a lie then that **MUST mean we are saved on WORKS ... Right? Thats** [sic] **not what the Word says.** (cap emphasis and ellipsis his)

> I just ran across your web site. It saddened me to realize that not only are you probably unsaved, but that you are actively evangelizing for Satan. You do not have to hate Christ just bacause [sic] you have rejected His grace. However, you would be better off if you **accepted Christ as your Savior, and stopped believing in the power of your works as your savior in lieu of Christ, or in addition to Christ.**

Such an inference could not be further from the truth! This misrepresentation seems to be given by many to immediately discredit, negate and dismiss what is taught about **the necessity to faithfully endure in heart purity and through persecution until the end of one's life for salvation's sake** (Rev. 2:10,11; Mt. 5:8; 10:22; Heb. 3:14; etc.).

No Scripture

First, **nowhere does the Bible say if one rejects OSAS that he is believing in a *works salvation*.** Nowhere. **When a Christian rejects the teaching of OSAS, he does so because of Biblical grounds.** No one would want to not believe in OSAS if it wasn't for the message of the Scriptures. In fact, there are so many Scriptures that refute OSAS that it would be difficult to list all of them. Such Scriptures are found from Genesis through Revelation. (Please consult our 801 page book entitled, *The Believer's Conditional Security* for proof. This book is available through Evangelical Outreach, PO Box 265, Washington, PA 15301.)

Christians Are Disheartened By OSAS

Second, many Christians are greatly disheartened by the teaching of OSAS, because they know that certain sins can bring a righteous man to his spiritual death, and therefore, can see the danger in this doctrine. Some of the Scripture references are:

> Don't you know that when you offer yourselves to someone to obey him as slaves, you are slaves to the one whom you obey—whether you are slaves to **sin, which leads to death**, or to obedience, which leads to righteousness? (Rom 6:16)

> For **if you live according to the sinful nature, you will die**; but if by the Spirit you put to death the misdeeds of the body, you will live. (Rom 8:13)

> But each one is tempted when, by his own evil desire, he is dragged away and enticed. Then, after desire has conceived, it gives birth to sin; and **sin, when it is full-grown, gives birth to death. Don't be deceived, my dear brothers.** (James 1:14-16)

> For this son of mine **was dead** and **is alive again**; he **was lost** and is found. So they began to celebrate. (Luke 15:24)

> My brethren, **if any among you strays from the truth and one turns him back**, let him know that he who turns a sinner from the

error of his way will **save his soul from death** and will cover a multitude of sins. (James 5:19,20)

The acts of the sinful nature are obvious: sexual immorality, impurity and debauchery; idolatry and witchcraft; hatred, discord, jealousy, fits of rage, selfish ambition, dissensions, factions and envy; drunkenness, orgies, and the like. **I warn you, as I did before, that those who live like this will not inherit the kingdom of God.** (Gal 5:19-21)

If I tell the righteous man that he will surely live, but then he trusts in his righteousness and does evil, none of the righteous things he has done will be remembered; **he will die for the evil he has done.** (Ezek 33:13)

Again, it's not, therefore, that Christians who oppose OSAS are teaching a *works salvation* as often accused, but that they know the basic Scriptural truth about sin's deadly spiritual effects on the soul of the righteous, which is flatly denied by OSAS teachers.

Not an *Original* Teaching

Third, Christians who teach that sexual immorality, drunkenness, theft, greed, witchcraft, and the like (see Mt. 5:28,29;1 Cor. 6:9,10; Rev. 21:8; 22:15) will exclude all such people from God's kingdom are not teaching anything of their own making. All we are doing is citing what Jesus and His Apostles taught, as found in the Bible. If we are guilty of teaching a *works salvation,* then they taught that as well, which is impossible. In fact, such a teaching is under the umbrella of *grace,* in contrast to what many have been believing.

Grace Has Been Dangerously Distorted

Fourth, it appears that one of the main reasons why this strawman argument of a *works salvation* accusation is given is because *grace* **has been presented as a *license for immorality* for so long, and without challenge, that it seems strange to people in our day to hear the real truth, even if it is directly read from the Bible!** It is shocking to see the spiritual blindness that holds the OSAS people in this dangerous deception. Again, *grace* has been grossly and dangerously misrepresented by the trusted spiritual reputed leaders of our dark hour. The most detailed explanation of God's *grace* which brings *salvation* is found in the following rarely quoted Scripture:

> For **the grace of God that brings salvation** has appeared to all men. It teaches us **to say "No" to ungodliness and worldly passions, and to live self-controlled, upright and godly lives in this present age.** (Titus 2:11,12)

In contrast to the truth, *grace* **is distorted and changed by OSAS teachers into something which gives** *allowance* **or** *permission* **for immorality, though the OSAS teachers will certainly deny this. Bob George, Charles Stanley, Chuck Swindoll, as well as many others, have been openly teaching this way, while other OSAS teachers are sometimes more subtle about this same impression they leave their listeners with.** The real truth is that Biblical grace is equated to *holiness* and never gives allowance for wickedness, even in our modern society. **It is too bad that Titus 2:11,12 aren't used in their proper context and cited as frequently as we have heard Eph. 2:8,9 and John 3:16.** But how could they be, since we continue to suffer under the influence of the OSAS teachers?

We Are Saved by *Grace* Not by *Works* And We *Warn* The *Righteous*

Fifth, please know that I and many other Christians believe we are saved by *grace* and *not by works*. **We, however, also know that** *sin* **can bring a true Christian (a** *righteous* **man) to his [spiritual] death, as already mentioned. Hence, we warn the** *righteous* **in a way the OSAS teachers** *never* **could:**

> Again, **when a righteous man** turns from his righteousness and does evil, and I put a stumbling block before him, he will **die**. Since you did not **warn** him, he will **die for his sin.** The righteous things he did will not be remembered, and I will hold you accountable for his **blood.** (Ezek 3:20)

A Watchman's Responsibility To Sound The *Trumpet*

Warning all people about sin is like sounding a *trumpet* of warning:

Son of man, speak to your countrymen and say to them: When I bring the sword against a land, and the people of the land choose one of their men and make him their watchman, and he sees the sword coming against the land and **blows the trumpet to warn the people**, then if anyone hears the trumpet but does not take warning and the sword comes and takes his life, **his blood will be on his own head**. Since he heard the sound of the trumpet but did not take warning, his **blood** will be on his own head. If he had taken warning, he would have saved himself. But if the watchman sees the sword coming and **does not blow the trumpet to warn the people** and the sword comes and takes the life of one of them, that man will be taken away because of his sin, but **I will hold the watchman accountable for his blood**. Son of man, I have made you a watchman for the house of Israel; so hear the word I speak and give them warning from me. When I say to the wicked, "O wicked man, you will surely die," and you do not speak out to dissuade him from his ways, that wicked man will die for his sin, and **I will hold you accountable for his blood ... If a righteous man turns** from his righteousness and does evil, he will **die** for it. And **if a wicked man turns** away from his wickedness and does what is just and right, he will **live** by doing so. (Ezek 33:2-8, 18, 19)

Sinful Israel didn't like God's *way* about the righteous turning to evil and dying spiritually so they rejected it, like many from the OSAS point of view do in our day:

Yet, O house of Israel, you say, "The way of the Lord is not just." But I will judge each of you according to his own ways. But if **a wicked man turns** away from all the sins he has committed and keeps all my decrees and does what is just and right, he will surely live; **he will not die**. None of the offenses he has committed will be remembered against him. Because of the righteous things he has done, **he will live**. Do I take any pleasure in the death of the wicked? declares the Sovereign LORD. Rather, am I not pleased when they turn from their ways and live? But if **a righteous man turns** from his righteousness and commits sin and does the same detestable things the wicked man does, will he live? None of the righteous things he has done will be remembered. Because of the unfaithfulness he is guilty of and because of the sins he has committed, **he will die. Yet**

you say, "The way of the Lord is not just." Hear, O house of Israel: Is my way unjust? Is it not your ways that are unjust? **If a righteous man turns from his righteousness and commits sin, he will die for it; because of the sin he has committed he will die. But if a wicked man turns away from the wickedness he has committed and does what is just and right, he will save his life. Because he considers all the offenses he has committed and turns away from them, he will surely live; he will not die.** Yet the house of Israel says, "The way of the Lord is not just." Are my ways unjust, O house of Israel? Is it not your ways that are unjust? Therefore, O house of Israel, I will judge you, each one according to his ways, declares the Sovereign LORD. Repent! **Turn away from all your offenses; then sin will not be your downfall.** Rid yourselves of all the offenses you have committed, and get a new heart and a new spirit. **Why will you die**, O house of Israel? For I take no pleasure in the death of anyone, declares the Sovereign LORD. **Repent and live!** (Ezek 18:20-32)

The context of this passage shows Ezekiel wrote about *spiritual death for the righteous man who turns away* and not physical death, since the contrast says if a wicked man turns away from wickedness **he will live** and **not** *die.* Yet the same ones who did *not die* [spiritually] did die physically. Therefore, *spiritual death* is under discussion and **not physical death**, like some would distort the meaning to say.

Because He Took Warning

A righteous man will continue to live spiritually *only* **because he took warning** not to sin because he would *die* and, therefore, refrained. **Such a warning is vital for the godly, as well as sparing ourselves from** *blood* **guilt, according to the Scriptures.** Again, notice this Scripture:

Again, when a righteous man turns from his righteousness and does evil, and I put a stumbling block before him, **he will die.** Since you did not **warn** him, he **will die for his sin.** The righteous things he did will not be remembered, and I will hold you accountable for his blood. But if you do **warn the righteous man** not to sin and he does not sin, he will surely live **because he took warning**, and you will have saved yourself. (Ezek 3:20,21)

What a terrible disadvantage, therefore, a Christian places himself under just by listening to any OSAS teacher, pastor, evangelist, etc., **because he will never hear this type of all-important warning.**

I Will Hold You Accountable for His Blood

Please notice once again the striking words *because he took warning* in Ezek 3:21. They are very important, for they show that a warning of this magnitude **can be a life sustaining blessing for Christians, who heed that warning. Not only don't the OSAS teachers issue such a** *warning*, **they actually** *deny* **the truth of this passage because of their OSAS doctrine. Remember, the Apostle Paul knew that** *blood* **guilt was a real possibility for him under New Testament** *grace:*

> But when the Jews opposed Paul and became abusive, he shook out his clothes in protest and said to them, **"Your blood be on your own heads!** I am clear of **my responsibility.** From now on I will go to the Gentiles." (Acts 18:6)

> Therefore, I declare to you today that I am innocent of **the blood of all men.** For I have not hesitated to proclaim to you the whole will of God. (Acts 20:26,27)

I will hold you accountable for his blood, **as found in Ezekiel, are words that Paul took seriously as a Christian, as all Christians should today. In contrast, very few seem to even know this** *responsibility* **applies under God's true** *grace.* **Also, to proclaim** *the whole will of God* **must include our personal responsibility of warning both the** *righteous* **and** *wicked* **of sin's deadly effects on the soul. May Almighty God open the eyes of multitudes to these basic Christian truths before even more people end up in the eternal, unquenchable and raging fires of hell because of OSAS.**

16

The Lord Repeated This Salvation Truth Six Times

Every word in the Bible is precious, important and has eternal consequences. How vital it is to read and act upon Jesus' dialog with Nicodemas where the Lord mentions the necessity of getting *born again* to enter the kingdom of God (John 3:3-7). And let's not forget the Lord's teaching regarding lust in the heart being *adultery* (Mt. 5:28). But both of these arresting teachings are only found *once* in the Scriptures.

Furthermore, how filled with priceless insights is the *Parable of the Sower*, which is repeated *three* different times in the Gospel accounts, unlike some other Parables which are found once.

Few teachings of the Lord are found more than three times, but **one particular teaching is found *six* times in all four Gospel accounts and is related to the believer's security (salvation). Certainly this reiteration reflects its importance. It is Jesus' repeated teaching about *losing* one's *life* (or *soul*).** Again, such emphasis reflects glaring truth which should not be quickly passed over. Let's take a close look at these six Scriptures and also remember that **almost all of them were spoken directly to the disciples, those who had already experienced initial salvation. Moreover, all six Scriptures contain first a warning and then a *safeguard* regarding salvation:**

Matthew 10:39

1. Whoever **finds his life** will lose it, and whoever **loses his life** for my sake will find it. (Mt 10:39)

The Greek word for *life* is always *psuche* in these Scriptures and translated *soul* once. The word itself means:

heart (+ *-ily*), *life, mind, soul,* + *us*, + *you*.

Psuche is used in other Scriptures and in various ways, such as the following ones:

I am the good shepherd. The good shepherd lays down his **life** for the sheep. (John 10:11)

Now my **heart** is troubled, and what shall I say? "Father, save me from this hour"? No, it was for this very reason I came to this hour. (John 12:27)

But the Jews who refused to believe stirred up the Gentiles and poisoned their **minds** against the brothers. (Acts 14:2)

men who have risked their **lives** for the name of our Lord Jesus Christ. (Acts 15:26)

However, I consider my **life** worth nothing to me, if only I may finish the race and complete the task the Lord Jesus has given me—the task of testifying to the gospel of God's grace. (Acts 20:24)

What good is it for a man to gain the whole world, yet forfeit his **soul**? Or what can a man give in exchange for his **soul**? (Mk 8:36,37)

Certainly, Jesus is teaching we must be willing to die physically, if necessary, for the cause of Christ in Mt. 10:39. Note the context:

Anyone who loves his father or mother more than me is not worthy of me; anyone who loves his son or daughter more than me is not worthy of me; and anyone who does not take his cross and follow me is not worthy of me. Whoever **finds his life will lose it,** and whoever **loses his life for my sake will find it.** (Mt 10:37-39)

To *lose* your soul, all you have to do as a Christian is to *find* your life (*psuche*).

Matthew 16:25 and Luke 9:24

The second and third times Jesus gave this teaching are found at Mt. 16:25 and Luke 9:24. Respectively they read:

2. For whoever **wants to save his life will lose it,** but whoever **loses his life** for me will find it.

3. For whoever **wants to save his life will lose it,** but whoever **loses his life** for me will save it.

Here, loss of salvation will come if one *wants to save his life.*

Mark 8:35

The context of Mk. 8:35 is most revealing:

4. For whoever wants to **save his life** (psuche) will lose it, but whoever **loses his life** (psuche) for me **and for the gospel** will save it. For what shall it profit a man, if he shall gain the whole world, and lose his own **soul** (psuche)? Or what shall a man give in exchange for his **soul** (psuche)? (Mk 8:35-37)

Soul is used in verses 36 and 37 to clarify that **it is the *soul* of man that can be *lost*,** which is especially clear when pondering verses 35 through 37 together. This shows the warning Jesus gave in these four Scriptures (with two more coming) is related to *salvation* itself and nothing less. **Mark 8:35-37 was spoken to a mixed crowd of people, both saved and unsaved. Hence, Jesus wanted those saved to know they could yet become lost just like he wanted those still on the road to hell to know the price God demands for final salvation (an actual entrance into God's kingdom).**

Luke 17:33

5. Whoever tries to **keep his life** will lose it, and whoever **loses his life** will **preserve** it. (Luke 17:33)

This passage spoken to the disciples is the first and only time of the six passages that Jesus used the word translated *preserve*. The Greek meaning is *to rescue from death*. The Lord spoke this to his disciples and hence, told them how to *rescue from death* their own *souls*.

A Christian is told by Jesus to walk with the willingness to die as a *martyr* at any time. Compare to Acts 1:8:

> But you will receive power when the Holy Spirit comes on you; and you will be my **witnesses** in Jerusalem, and in all Judea and Samaria, and to the ends of the earth.

(The word translated *witnesses* is the one from which we get the word *martyr*.) A Christian will preserve his own salvation by walking in this attitude of mind. Paul wrote:

> And as for us, why do we endanger ourselves every hour? **I die every day**—I mean that, brothers—just as surely as I glory over you in Christ Jesus our Lord. (1 Cor 15:30,31)

John 12:25

6.   The man who **loves his life** will lose it, while the man who **hates his life** (psuche) in this world will keep it for **eternal life.** (John 12:25)

With crystal clarity this verse shows that we must *hate* our life (psuche) in this world to keep it for *eternal life* (or salvation). Of these six Scriptures Mark 8:35-37 and John 12:25 are most clear to show **salvation** is the subject.

Jesus also spoke of *hating* our life for salvation's sake at another time:

> If anyone comes to me and does not **hate** his father and mother, his wife and children, his brothers and sisters—yes, even his own **life** (psuche)—he **cannot be my disciple.** (Luke 14:26)

In Luke 14:26, the Lord stated that a stipulation to be his disciple is to *hate* **your** *life* (psuche), which coincides with his teaching in John 12:25 to *keep* it for eternal life (zoe). According to Jesus, this is a condition to be his disciple. So again, since to be a *disciple* means being a Christian (Mt.

12:49,50), then we have yet another verse showing that this is all a salvation issue, according to the Lord Himself.

The word *miseo* translated *hate* found here, as well as in John 12:25, means:

> to detest (espec. to persecute); by extens. to love less:—hate (-ful).

The context of John 12:25 is as follows:

> Philip went to tell Andrew; Andrew and Philip in turn told Jesus. Jesus replied, "The hour has come for the Son of Man to be glorified. I tell you the truth, unless a kernel of wheat falls to the ground and dies, it remains only a single seed. But if it dies, it produces many seeds. **The man who loves his life will lose it, while the man who hates his life in this world will keep it for eternal life.** Whoever serves me must follow me; and where I am, my servant also will be. My Father will honor the one who serves me." (John 12:22-26)

(**John 12.25** is one of the passages on *eternal life,* that most don't even know exists, just like **Gal. 6:8**.)

We must *Hate* our Life in This World To Stay Saved

The Lord himself said for us to *keep* our life **we must *hate* it in this world.** If a Christian comes to *love* his life now, he will *lose* it. What an important Scripture. Please compare that to the following one:

> If only for this life we have hope in Christ, we are to be pitied more than all men. (1 Cor 15:19)

The ultimate spiritual danger of a Christian going to hell still exists, and that is by him coming to *find, save, keep* and/or *love* his *psuche* in this world now and therefore not *preserve* or *keep it for eternal life.*

The Christian will *only* remain saved by *losing* and/or *hating* his *psuche* now for Jesus and the gospel, according to these verses. (Notice how the *gospel* is placed alongside of Jesus himself regarding its importance. The Christian *gospel* includes a conditional security for the believer,

1 Cor. 15:2.) We have to *love* Jesus more than our own lives and our families to be *worthy* of him, that is, to be a Christian.

Stephen is a prime example of one willing to die for the gospel, just like we need to be! Can you identify with him regarding his willingness to die physically for the Lord and the gospel message? No doubt, he was carrying his cross and following Jesus faithfully to the end.

The Christian will *save, preserve* and/or *keep* his soul by *losing* and/or *hating* his life now, according to Jesus. (By comparing these 6 Scriptures to and with themselves this is our deduction.)

Remember eternal life for a Christian (besides being a present-tense possession) is also a *promise* (1 John 2:24,25), something we enter into at the end of this age (Mk. 10:30) and after the sheep/goat judgment (Mt. 25:46), if we are faithful overcomers (Rev. 2:10,11) and if we *continue* to sow to please the Spirit of God and don't give up (Gal. 6:8,9).

To disown Jesus to save yourself from physical death or persecution now is a prime example of saving your *life* but losing it. This is clear proof that the Apostles all temporarily lost their salvation when they disowned Him for fear of their lives. See also Mt. 10:33. They regained their salvation afterwards.

Again, according to Jesus, a Christian will lose his salvation if he *finds, saves, keeps* and/or *loves his life.*

Those that stay saved, according to these safeguards from the Lord, *lose their life for* Jesus *and the gospel* as well as *hate* their *life in this world.* This is how the Christian can *find, save, keep* and *preserve* his salvation. (It is also apparent from John 12:25 that the Lord was teaching on salvation by the words *eternal life.*)

"Get a Life"?

One final point: Who knows how many times the godly have heard the wicked say to them *Get a life.* According to Jesus, if such would occur the follower of Jesus would lose his salvation. Hence, such darkened people are speaking for the devil though they probably don't know it. The truth is: It is only the godly who have spiritual *life* while the wicked remain *dead* in their sins.

17

How Will A Christian Die Because Of Sin?

Paul taught Christians the following:

> For **if you live according to the sinful nature, you will die**; but if by the Spirit you put to death the misdeeds of the body, you will live. (Rom 8:13)

Some say this *death* is physical death, while others say it is spiritual death, like the kind Adam and Eve experienced after they sinned. Is there a way we can know for certain? By comparing Scripture with Scripture we can know what he is referring to. On three different occasions Paul taught Christians what would happen to them if they would live according to the flesh (or sinful nature)—the one just cited in Rom. 8:13 and the following two:

> The acts of the sinful nature are obvious: sexual immorality, impurity and debauchery; idolatry and witchcraft; hatred, discord, jealousy, fits of rage, selfish ambition, dissensions, factions and envy; drunkenness, orgies, and the like. I warn you, as I did before, that **those who live like this will not inherit the kingdom of God.** (Gal 5:19-21)

> **The one who sows to please his sinful nature, from that nature will reap destruction;** the one who sows to please the Spirit, from the Spirit will reap eternal life. (Gal 6:8)

By comparing these passages, we can see that Paul warns Christians they will "die" by living according to the sinful nature (Rom. 8:13); "**not inherit the kingdom of God**" if they live out the acts of the sinful nature (Gal. 5:19-21) and "**reap destruction**" in contrast to "eternal life" by sowing to please the sinful nature (Gal. 6:8). In other words, the "die" of Rom. 8:13 is the same as "not inherit[ing] the kingdom of God" in Gal. 5:19-21 and the "reap[ing of] destruction" of Gal. 6:8. If A=B and B=C, then A=C. This also sheds important light on what it means not to *inherit* the kingdom of God as also mentioned in 1 Cor. 6:9,10. Clearly then not to inherit the kingdom of God means to reap destruction and not *eternal life*. This is a good refutation to Stanley, Evans and others who think you can enter God's kingdom but not inherit God's kingdom.

Hence, by comparing these Scriptures, we know Paul taught Christians they will "die" *spiritually*, if they live according to the sinful nature. James also declared the exact same truth:

> But each one is tempted when, by his own evil desire, he is dragged away and enticed. Then, after desire has conceived, it gives birth to sin; and **sin, when it is full-grown, gives birth to death. Don't be deceived**, my dear brothers. (James 1:14-16)

This is also what God had informed mankind from the very beginning on down through the centuries:

> And the LORD God commanded the man, "You are free to eat from any tree in the garden; but you must not eat from the tree of the knowledge of good and evil, for when you eat of it **you will surely die.**" (Gen 2:16,17)

> **If a righteous man** turns from his righteousness and does evil, **he will die for it.** (Ezek 33:18)

> Don't you know that when you offer yourselves to someone to obey him as slaves, you are slaves to the one whom you obey—**whether you are slaves to sin, which leads to death**, or to obedience, which leads to righteousness? (Rom 6:16)

While sin leads to spiritual death, a faith in Jesus which produces holiness and obedience results in eternal life:

But now that you have been set free from sin and have become slaves to God, the benefit you reap leads to holiness, and the result is **eternal life**. For **the wages of sin is death**, but the gift of God is eternal life in Christ Jesus our Lord. (Rom 6:22,23)

To those who by persistence in doing good seek glory, honor and immortality, he will give **eternal life**. (Rom 2:7)

...the one who sows to please the Spirit, from the Spirit will reap **eternal life**. (Gal 6:8)

Though this is what the original Christians taught and believed themselves, in our day the aforementioned truths have been opposed and flatly denied by the eternal security teachers. Friends, as James wrote, "**Don't be deceived**, my dear brothers" (1:16).

18

From Sanctified To Enemies Of God

There are many ways to disprove the teaching of eternal security. The following passage is one of many which does this:

> If we deliberately keep on sinning after we have received the knowledge of the truth, no sacrifice for sins is left, but only a fearful expectation of judgment and of **raging fire that will consume the enemies of God.** Anyone who rejected the law of Moses died without mercy on the testimony of two or three witnesses. How much more severely do you think a man deserves to be punished who has trampled the Son of God under foot, who has treated as an unholy thing **the blood of the covenant that sanctified him,** and who has insulted the Spirit of grace? For we know him who said, "It is mine to avenge; I will repay," and again, "The Lord will judge his people." It is a dreadful thing to fall into the hands of the living God. (Heb 10:26-31)

Most importantly, notice that the passage is about those who were **once *sanctified* by the blood of Jesus**. Once when sharing this devastating passage with an eternal security proponent, he said to me that it wasn't the blood of Jesus but the blood of bulls and goats that sanctified them! That statement is erroneous in two ways: (1) The contrast in Heb. 10:26-31 is between the law of Moses and the new covenant. Hence, **Jesus' blood is the means whereby the people are sanctified**, and not the blood of bulls and goats. (2) Scripture is very clear in stating Jesus' blood sanctifies:

Therefore **Jesus also, that He might sanctify the people through His own blood,** suffered outside the gate. (Heb 13:12, NASB)

(The same Greek word for *sanctify* is used at Heb. 10:29 and Heb. 13:12.) **Also, notice that the same ones who were *sanctified* [past tense] also *trampled the Son of God under foot*. This again shows we are not talking about the old covenant but the new. These same people became *enemies of God* from their former condition of being *sanctified* and that was because of sin.** Clearly, their future sins were not forgiven even before they were committed like some say, neither were they viewed by God as the righteousness of Christ when in these sins! Moreover, neither the seal of the Holy Spirit, nor anything else offered as unconditional protection by the eternal security advocate prevented this horrible spiritual reversal. Furthermore, **those who were once sanctified by Jesus' blood were now headed for *raging fire*. There was no eternal security for them and there is no eternal security for us.** The sooner we accept this fact, the sooner we can walk in a more guarded manner in this world which has claimed many spiritual casualties among those who were once truly God's children.

For much more information on this subject, please consult our book, *The Believer's Conditional Security.*

19

The Real Importance
Of Obedience To God

I have no doubt some people will read this chapter's heading and conclude from that alone that the author might be in legalism, a "work's salvation," or is in some kind of *cultic* doctrine. According to today's version of
grace, obedience to God is optional and, therefore, not even a priority for
many. But is that the real truth or a lie from the devil, who is trying to
damn your soul to Hell through false teachings, which come from the devil's servants? Before you prejudge this chapter, please carefully ponder the
following Scriptures given by the Lord Jesus Himself and His disciples and
adjust your behavior and theology accordingly for your own benefit.

Jesus told the Apostles to *go and make disciples* and teach those new
disciples to *obey* everything they were commanded.

> Therefore go and make disciples of all nations, baptizing them in the
> name of the Father and of the Son and of the Holy Spirit, and teach-
> ing them to **obey** everything I have commanded you. And surely I am
> with you always, to the very end of the age. (Mat 28:19,20)

Jesus corrected a woman who praised Mary his mother just because
she gave birth to him and then declared the *blessed* people are those who
obey God's word.

> As Jesus was saying these things, a woman in the crowd called out,
> "Blessed is the mother who gave you birth and nursed you." He re-
> plied, "Blessed rather are those who hear the word of God and **obey**
> it." (Luke 11:27,28)

We show our *love* for Jesus and God by *obedience.*

If you love me, you will **obey** what I command. (John 14:15)

Whoever has my commands and **obeys** them, he is the one who loves me. He who loves me will be loved by my Father, and I too will love him and show myself to him. (John 14:21)

This is love for God: to **obey** his commands. And his commands are not burdensome. (1 John 5:3)

Love or non-love for Jesus is reflected in our *obedience* to Jesus' teachings.

Jesus replied, "If anyone loves me, he will **obey** my teaching. My Father will love him, and we will come to him and make our home with him. He who does not love me will not **obey** my teaching. These words you hear are not my own; they belong to the Father who sent me. (John 14:23, 24)

Those that actually inherit the kingdom of God *love* (or obey) God.

Listen, my dear brothers: Has not God chosen those who are poor in the eyes of the world to be rich in faith and to inherit the kingdom he promised **those who love him**? (James 2:5)

To remain in Jesus' love, we must meet the condition of *obeying* his commands.

If you **obey** my commands, you will remain in my love, just as I have obeyed my Father's commands and remain in his love. (John 15:10)

Jesus' servants *obey* today just like they did back in Jesus' days on Earth.

Remember the words I spoke to you: "No servant is greater than his master." If they persecuted me, they will persecute you also. If they obeyed my teaching, they will **obey** yours also. (John 15:20)

The Apostles knew they and others could and should *obey* God.

> Peter and the other apostles replied: "We must **obey** God rather than men!" (Acts 5:29)

> As they traveled from town to town, they delivered the decisions reached by the apostles and elders in Jerusalem for the people to **obey.** (Acts 16:4)

> But now revealed and made known through the prophetic writings by the command of the eternal God, so that all nations might believe and **obey** him. (Rom 16:26)

> Therefore, my dear friends, as you have always **obeyed**—not only in my presence, but now much more in my absence—**continue to work out your salvation with fear and trembling.** (Phil 2:12)

The Holy Spirit is given to people who *obey* God.

> We are witnesses of these things, and so is the Holy Spirit, whom God has given to those who **obey** him. (Acts 5:32)

We are slaves to sin or to *obedience* depending on whom we *obey*.

> Don't you know that when you offer yourselves to someone to **obey** him as slaves, you are slaves to the one whom you **obey**—whether you are slaves to sin, which leads to death, or to obedience, which leads to righteousness? But thanks be to God that, though you used to be slaves to sin, you wholeheartedly **obeyed** the form of teaching to which you were entrusted. You have been set free from sin and have become slaves to righteousness. (Rom 6:16-18)

The gospel is to be *obeyed* for salvation's sake.

> He will punish those who do not know God and do not **obey** the gospel of our Lord Jesus. They will be punished with everlasting destruction and shut out from the presence of the Lord and from the majesty of his power. (2 Th 1:8,9)

Those who have salvation *obey* God.

> And, once made perfect, he became the source of eternal salvation for all who **obey** him. (Heb 5:9)

> Those who **obey** his commands live in him, and he in them. And this is how we know that he lives in us: We know it by the Spirit he gave us. (1 John 3:24)

The unsaved are described here as those who don't *obey* the gospel.

> For it is time for judgment to begin with the family of God; and if it begins with us, what will the outcome be for those who **do not obey** the gospel of God? (1 Pet 4:17)

Obedience to God's commands is a proof of salvation. **Those who claim salvation, but don't *obey* are liars.**

> We know that we have come to know him if we **obey** his commands. **The man who says, "I know him," but does not do what he commands is a liar, and the truth is not in him.** (1 John 2:3,4)

Prayer assurance for a Christian is based on his *obedience*. One command has especially been singled out.

> And receive from him anything we ask, because we **obey** his commands and do what pleases him. And this is his command: **to believe in the name of his Son, Jesus Christ, and to love one another as he commanded us.** (1 John 3:22,23)

> And now, dear lady, I am not writing you a new command but one we have had from the beginning. I ask that we love one another. And this is love: that **we walk in obedience to his commands.** As you have heard from the beginning, his command is that you walk in love. (2 John 1:5,6)

Jesus' commands are to be *obeyed.*

Remember, therefore, what you have received and heard; **obey** it, and repent. But if you do not wake up, I will come like a thief, and you will not know at what time I will come to you. (Rev 3:3)

Christians are described, in part, as those who *obey* God's commandments.

Then the dragon was enraged at the woman and went off to make war against the rest of her offspring—those who **obey** God's commandments and **hold to the testimony of Jesus.** (Rev 12:17)

This calls for patient endurance on the part of the saints who **obey** God's commandments and **remain faithful to Jesus.** (Rev 14:12)

A Christian's *obedience* comes from his faith (in Jesus Christ).

Through him and for his name's sake, we received grace and apostleship to call people from among all the Gentiles to **the obedience that comes from faith.** (Rom. 1:5)

From all of these Scriptures, we have a clear picture that **true Christians can and do *obey* God's commandments and are not living immorally as multitudes of false teachers, such as those that teach eternal security, say does occur.** Disobedience can bring forth spiritual death to a person who was once saved (Lk. 15:24,32; Rom. 6:16; 8:13; James 1:14,15; 5:19,20; etc.) Ponder the following Scriptures that clarify this and do not let yourself be deceived:

For God did not call us to be impure, but to live a holy life. Therefore, he who rejects this instruction does not **reject** man but **God,** who gives you his Holy Spirit. (1 Thess. 4:7,8)

For of this you can be sure: No immoral, impure or greedy person—such a man is an idolater—**has any inheritance in the kingdom of Christ and of God. Let no one deceive you with empty words,** for because of such things God's wrath comes on those who are disobedient. Therefore do not be partners with them. (Eph. 5:5-7)

Do you not know that **the wicked will not inherit the kingdom of God? Do not be deceived: Neither** the sexually immoral nor idolaters nor adulterers nor male prostitutes nor homosexuals nor thieves nor the greedy nor drunkards nor slanderers nor swindlers **will inherit the kingdom of God.** (1 Cor. 6:9,10)

But the cowardly, the unbelieving, the vile, the murderers, the sexually immoral, those who practice magic arts, the idolaters and all liars —**their place will be in the fiery lake of burning sulfur.** This is the second death. (Rev. 21:8)

The acts of the sinful nature are obvious: sexual immorality, impurity and debauchery; idolatry and witchcraft; hatred, discord, jealousy, fits of rage, selfish ambition, dissensions, factions and envy; drunkenness, orgies, and the like. **I warn you, as I did before, that those who live like this will not inherit the kingdom of God.** (Gal. 5:19-21)

The one who sows to please his sinful nature, from that nature **will reap destruction**; the one who sows to please the Spirit, from the Spirit **will reap eternal life.** Let us not become weary in doing good, for at the proper time we will reap a harvest if we do not give up. (Gal. 6:8,9)

And remember this, Jesus described his true spiritual family (his disciples) as those who put into *practice* God's word and do his will.

He replied, "My mother and brothers are those who hear God's word and **put it into practice.**" (Luke 8:21)

Pointing to **his disciples**, he said, "**Here are my mother and my brothers. For whoever does the will of my Father in heaven is my brother and sister and mother.**" (Mat. 12:49,50)

He also stated that one is *a wise builder* or *a foolish builder* based on the single condition of putting into *practice* the word of God.

Therefore everyone who hears these words of mine and **puts them into practice** is like a wise man who built his house on the rock. The rain came down, the streams rose, and the winds blew and beat against that house; yet it did not fall, because it had its foundation on the rock. But everyone who hears these words of mine and **does not put them into practice** is like a foolish man who built his house on sand. The rain came down, the streams rose, and the winds blew and beat against that house, and it fell with a great crash. (Mat. 7:24-27)

Friend, the real importance about your *obedience* to God and the seriousness of disobedience (sin) is partly shown by these Bible verses. Reject all who teach otherwise, even if they are popular. To help reinforce the aforementioned eternal truths, please reread these Scriptures and pass them on to others. **Do not be deceived by an eternal security teacher.**

20

"That The Spirit May Be Saved"

1 Cor. 5:1-5 (KJV) read:

> It is reported commonly that there is **fornication** among you, and such fornication as is not so much as named among the Gentiles, that one should have his father's wife. And ye are puffed up, and have not rather mourned, that he that hath done this deed might be taken away from among you. For I verily, as absent in body, but present in spirit, have judged already, as though I were present, concerning him that hath so done this deed, In the name of our Lord Jesus Christ, when ye are gathered together, and my spirit, with the power of our Lord Jesus Christ, To deliver such an one unto Satan **for the destruction of the flesh, that the spirit may be saved in the day of the Lord Jesus.**

Many people cite this passage to support their belief in once saved always saved (OSAS). Notice the words "that the spirit may be saved." Have you ever wondered how that could mean "saved at that moment," as the OSAS proponents understand it? (I certainly have.) If **"may be saved"** in 1 Cor. 5:5 means "saved at that moment," then in 1 Cor. 10:33 it must mean the same. Let's look at that passage:

> Even as I please all men in all things, not seeking mine own profit, but the profit of many, that they **may be saved**. (1 Cor 10:33)

So then to be consistent with the OSAS understanding of 1 Cor. 5:5, "**may be saved**" in 1 Cor. 10:33 would mean that Paul suffered hatred, persecution and lack to spread the Gospel message and warn of the dangers of sin to first-time hearers because all the people were "saved at that moment." But does that make sense to you in light of the book of Acts? Hopefully, not. Why then do the OSAS people interpret 1 Cor. 5:5 that way?

Also, please notice that 1 Cor. 5:5 does NOT say the sexually immoral man was saved while in sexual immorality. Paul clearly identifies that same person as "**wicked**" in 1 Cor. 5:13. Please know that a "wicked" person is not a Christian on the road to heaven, as the OSAS teachers say. The same exact Greek word translated "wicked" in 1 Cor. 5:13 is found in Jesus' teaching and shows where such is headed:

> This is how it will be at the end of the age. The angels will come and separate the **wicked** from the righteous and throw them into **the fiery furnace**, where there will be weeping and gnashing of teeth. (Mat 13:49, 50)

Somehow the OSAS teachers have overlooked these facts to spread their **security-in-sin gospel**. Besides all of that information, the man of 1 Cor. 5:1-5 was guilty of fornication (sexual immorality). In other Scriptures, it is crystal clear that such people will not inherit the kingdom of God but will instead be thrown into the lake of fire. Please read for yourself Gal. 5:19-21; Rev. 21:8; Eph. 5:5-7; 1 Cor. 6:9,10; etc. Such people need to repent for salvation's sake.

To expose and refute the OSAS teachers is obeying the command cited in Jude 3,4 as well as other ones. We are not unloving to teach the truth and refute the OSAS heresy. **Remember Gal. 6:8 says "eternal life" not "rewards," as the OSAS teachers use it for.**

21

Does The Seal Of The Holy Spirit Guarantee Salvation?

The belief that the *seal* of the Holy Spirit is an unconditional guarantee that a Christian will enter heaven is very common among the once saved always saved (OSAS) people. The question is: Does this really mean as they teach it? The *seal* of the Spirit is mentioned in the following verses:

> And you also were included in Christ when you heard the word of truth, the gospel of your salvation. Having believed, you were marked in him with a *seal*, the promised Holy Spirit, who is a deposit guaranteeing our inheritance until the redemption of those who are God's possession—to the praise of his glory. (Eph 1:13,14)

> And do not grieve the Holy Spirit of God, with whom you were *sealed* for the day of redemption. (Eph 4:30)

First, nowhere does the Bible say here or anywhere else that the "seal" can't be broken. Please make a note of this. In fact, the same Greek word translated "seal" (sphragizo) is found elsewhere and the context shows the seal can be broken:

> So they went and made the tomb secure by putting a **seal** on the stone and posting the guard. (Mat 27:66)

Since that stone over Jesus' tomb was latter moved, and the seal didn't prevent that from happening, then we know such doesn't absolutely assure it can't occur, as OSAS teachers say. They assume something they can't prove, but don't teach it as an assumption.

Secondly, we know the seal of the Holy Spirit can be broken because people that were saved have afterwards lost their salvation either temporarily or permanently. Since they were previously saved, then they were also sealed. Yet that didn't prevent sin from bringing forth spiritual death, as many scriptures declare can occur (Gen. 2:17; Ezek. 33:13,18; Rom. 8:13; James 1:14-16; etc.). Some examples of people who lost their salvation are as follows (other examples are not cited here, but are in our book, *The Believer's Conditional Security*):

> Timothy, my son, I give you this instruction in keeping with the prophecies once made about you, so that by following them you may fight the good fight, **holding on to faith and a good conscience**. Some have rejected these and so have shipwrecked their faith. Among them are Hymenaeus and Alexander, whom I have handed over to Satan to be taught not to blaspheme. (1 Tim 1:18-20)

Paul, the true grace teacher, knew the same horrible fate that occurred to Hymenaeus and Alexander could also happen to Timothy (who was certainly sealed by the Holy Spirit). Paul consequently told him what he needed to do to prevent this from happening to himself. So, as Hymenaeus and Alexander shipwrecked their faith, Paul knew godly Timothy could also have this happen to him (just like any Christian can). Another example is also from 1 Tim.:

> The goal of this command is love, which comes from **a pure heart and a good conscience and a sincere faith**. Some have wandered away from these and turned to meaningless talk. (1 Tim 1:5,6)

Please be assured that the only way any person can ever come to "a pure heart and a good conscience and a sincere faith" as Paul describes himself as having, is by a saving faith which contacts the blood of Christ. (Our hearts are purified by faith in Jesus, Acts 15:9.) Yet some people whom Paul knew (which he doesn't mention by name) "wandered away" from these (a pure heart and a good conscience and a sincere faith) and turned to "meaningless talk." Since one must have a pure heart to see God, and be holy (Mt. 5:8; Heb. 12:14; Rom. 6:22; etc.) and such can change after the point of salvation, then the seal of the Holy Spirit doesn't prevent this horrible thing from happening. Clearly then, Paul didn't think of the seal as the OSAS people do. **Please note also that Paul never said because those unnamed people turned from a pure heart and a good conscience and a sincere faith that it was proof they were never saved. (Some OSAS people argue like this at times but at other times they say saved people can turn to adultery and murder like King David did and still remain saved.)** What a heresy. So Paul, who wrote of the seal of the Holy Spirit in Eph. chapters 1 and 4, shows by these other scriptures what the seal meant to him. One doesn't have to go past the book of Ephesians to also get insight into this issue of the seal. Please ponder the following:

> For of this you can be sure: **No immoral, impure or greedy person —such a man is an idolater—has any inheritance in the kingdom of Christ and of God. Let no one deceive you with empty words,** for because of such things God's wrath comes on those who are disobedient. Therefore do not be partners with them. (Eph 5:5-7)

Paul wanted Christians, who were sealed with the Holy Spirit, to know that "No immoral, impure or greedy person—such a man is an idolater— has any inheritance in the kingdom of Christ and of God." In other words, he wanted them to know that the seal would not prevent those sins from nullifying their inheritance of the kingdom. Other Scriptures show that if you don't "inherit" the kingdom of God, you will go to the lake of fire (Rev. 21:1-8; Mt. 25:33-46; etc.). Hence, in the same breath that Paul wrote of the seal he warned Christians that sin could cause loss of salvation and the seal wouldn't prevent this. To teach otherwise is nothing more than "empty words," as Paul put it (Eph. 5:6).

22

False Prophets And False Teachers

According to the Lord Jesus, there are **"many"** false prophets in our present day that will **"deceive MANY people"** (Mt. 24:11). Though these false prophets might claim to know and communicate God's truth, they are spreading lies (Jer. 14:14). According to the loving Lord Jesus, false prophets are really hungry, dangerous, ferocious wolves dressed in sheep's clothing (Mt. 7:15). **Hence, they can be as spiritually deadly and dangerous to Christians (sheep—Jn. 10:27) as a concealed, savage wolf is among a flock of sheep!**

False prophets can be known by their "fruit" (Mt. 7:16), not their personal claims or "gifts." In fact, some false prophets can even produce miraculous signs (Mk. 13:22; Rev. 19:20) and accurately predict an event (Deut. 13:1-4). Other false prophets can be identified by their false prophecies made in the name of the LORD (Deut. 18:21,22). **In Jezebel's day, the false prophets feasted at the king's table (1 Ki. 18:19), while the true prophets were hid out in a cave and secretly fed there (1 Ki. 18:4). Popularity and affluence, therefore, must not be a criteria either when trying to identify a false prophet, since they sometimes have large followings.** False prophets speak with conviction, since they expect their lying words to be fulfilled (Ezek. 13:6). False teachers can also sound authoritative in their teachings (1 Tim. 1:7).

A New Testament example of a false prophet was Bar Jesus (Acts 13:6). As Paul was opposed by him, other servants of God in the past were likewise resisted by the popular false prophets in their day. Jeremiah is one such example (Jer. 26:7-15). Another was Micaiah, who was slapped in the face by a false prophet (1 Ki. 22:24). The misleading messages of false prophets can give comfort in vain (Zech. 10:2), fill sinful people with "false hopes" (Jer. 23:16), dress the wounds of sinful people as though they are not serious (Jer. 8:10, 11) and not expose the people's sins (Lam. 2:14). The false prophets, who had lying spirits that deceived Ahab, predicted success and victory in the name of the LORD (1 Ki. 22:11, 12). Because Ahab believed their message, he went into battle and died (22:35)! **Similarly, Paul predicted the day would come when a great number of teachers would be speaking what itching ears want to hear, not what they need to hear (the truth), as found in the Scriptures (2 Tim. 4:3).**

Again, "many" will be deceived by religious, innocent-looking-but-deadly enemies of Christianity, who bring the way of truth into disrepute (2 Pet. 2:1,2). **The Apostle Paul clearly stated that there are teachings which actually come from "demons" through false teachers (1 Tim. 4:1, 2) and that Satan has servants which masquerade as** *servants of righteousness* **(2 Cor. 11:15).** Though disturbing, these are facts!

To add to all of that, according to the Apostle John, it is actually possible to share in the wicked work of a false teacher:

> Anyone who runs ahead and does not continue in the teaching of Christ does not have God; whoever continues in the teaching has both the Father and the Son. If anyone comes to you and does not bring this teaching, do not take him into your house or welcome him. Anyone who welcomes him **shares in his wicked work.** (2 Jn. 9-11)

As we obey the command not to be gullible, but "test the spirits" (1 Jn. 4:1) so that we won't be deceived, we will have to **carefully evaluate teachers and ministries by the Scriptures**, which are always final authority (2 Tim. 3:16, 17).

Friend, Jesus wasn't joking when he said beware of false prophets that come to you in sheep's clothing but inwardly are ferocious wolves (Mt. 7:15). **They are here NOW!** Be on guard. It's a matter of life and death. Learn the Scriptures, so that you won't be deceived. **Eternity hangs in the balance.**

23

Vital Truths For New Converts

When a person becomes a true Christian he enters a brand new life. **In a moment of time he passes from death to life, from darkness to light and from the power of Satan to the power of God. Many things start to happen to him that may be surprising.** (I can still remember what it was like for me when I came to salvation over 25 years ago.) What you are going to read in this article is what I would have greatly benefitted by had I been presented with these vital Scriptural truths back then. **These are not the kinds of things you will readily hear from the typical** *pastor* **of our day or TV or radio teachers who seem more interested in getting people under their influence than spreading the word of life. Nonetheless, these eternal truths are precious pearls for the new convert.** Let's go to the Scriptures and see what they declare:

Family Division

Do not suppose that I have come to bring peace to the earth. I did not come to bring peace, but a sword. **For I have come to turn a man against his father, a daughter against her mother, a daughter-in-law against her mother-in-law—a man's enemies will be the members of his own household. Anyone who loves his father or mother more than me is not worthy of me; anyone who loves his son or daughter more than me is not worthy of me; and anyone who does not take his cross and follow me is not worthy of me.** Whoever finds his life will lose it, and whoever loses his life for my sake will find it. (Mat 10:34-39)

It is very common for one's family to be *divided* because of Christ, even to the point where dear family members become the new Christian's spiritual *enemies*. If this occurs to you, please know that it has also happened to multitudes of others as well. It is possible your unsaved family might want you to stop reading and talking about the Bible. They could also be ashamed of you being so *religious* all the time and will try to cool you down. Dear friend, regardless who or what might try to hinder your love, zeal and devotion to Jesus, **you must not yield to their ungodly desires**. You must love Jesus first, which will be shown by obeying him over others who would want you to go against the Lord's teachings or to just ignore them. This is vitally important. **To be *worthy* of Jesus, we must love him supremely**. Notice the following two Scriptures about those who *love* God:

> However, as it is written: "No eye has seen, no ear has heard, no mind has conceived what God has prepared for **those who love him**." (1 Cor 2:9)

> Listen, my dear brothers: Has not God chosen those who are poor in the eyes of the world to be rich in faith and **to inherit the kingdom he promised those who love him?** (James 2:5)

We show our love for God by obeying his commands (John 14:15).

Persecution

Another important fact of your new life in Christ is that you will bother people outside your family who don't have a heart for truth—old friends, coworkers, neighbors, etc. Some of these people will show their annoyance with persecution in various ways. Take heart and be encouraged by what Jesus (and Peter) taught:

> **Blessed are those who are persecuted because of righteousness, for theirs is the kingdom of heaven. Blessed are you when people insult you, persecute you and falsely say all kinds of evil against you because of me.** Rejoice and be glad, because great is your reward in heaven, for in the same way they persecuted the prophets who were before you. (Mat 5:10-12)

Blessed are you when men hate you, when they exclude you and insult you and reject your name as evil, because of the Son of Man. Rejoice in that day and leap for joy, because great is your reward in heaven. For that is how their fathers treated the prophets. (Luke 6:22,23)

They think it strange that **you do not plunge with them into the same flood of dissipation, and they heap abuse on you.** (1 Pet 4:4)

Persecution for righteousness, even in the milder form of being excluded or insulted, is a *test*. Loneliness is something all godly people have to deal with from time to time. Sadly, some Christians have *fallen away* from salvation over the test of persecution or just the fear of it:

... They believe for a while, but in the time of testing they fall away. (Luke 8:13)

So when (not if) persecution comes to you because you are living godly, continue to obey and let your light shine. But also remember not to cast your *pearls to swine*—those who boldly oppose the truth of God— because they may *tear you to pieces* (Mt. 7:6). Keep walking in faith thinking about the eternal rewards before you because of these persecutions. All godly people of the past were also persecuted and faced suffering:

In fact, everyone who wants to live a godly life in Christ Jesus **will be persecuted.** (2 Tim 3:12)

Others were tortured and refused to be released, so that they might gain a better resurrection. Some faced jeers and flogging, while still others were chained and put in prison. They were stoned; they were sawed in two; they were put to death by the sword. They went about in sheepskins and goatskins, destitute, persecuted and mistreated— **the world was not worthy of them.** They wandered in deserts and mountains, and in caves and holes in the ground. **These were all commended for their faith**, yet none of them received what had been promised. (Heb 11:35-39)

By faith Moses, when he had grown up, refused to be known as the son of Pharaoh's daughter. **He chose to be mistreated along with**

the people of God rather than to enjoy the pleasures of sin for a short time. He regarded disgrace for the sake of Christ as of greater value than the treasures of Egypt, because he was looking ahead to his reward. By faith he left Egypt, not fearing the king's anger; he persevered because he saw him who is invisible. (Heb 11:24-27)

We must be willing to die for Jesus if necessary and never be ashamed of Him or His words (Lk. 9:26).

The Importance of *Knowledge*

Similarly, Jesus taught:

All this I have told you **so that you will not go astray**. (John 16:1).

Hence, knowledge of certain things is a preventative from going *astray* or *stumbling*. Conversely, some do go astray because they are not aware of the things Jesus was referring to. Let's check the context to learn what the Lord is speaking of:

If the world hates you, keep in mind that it hated me first. If you be-longed to the world, it would love you as its own. As it is, you do not belong to the world, but I have chosen you out of the world. That is why the world hates you. Remember the words I spoke to you: "No servant is greater than his master." **If they persecuted me, they will persecute you also**. If they obeyed my teaching, they will obey yours also. They will treat you this way because of my name, for they do not know the One who sent me. If I had not come and spoken to them, they would not be guilty of sin. Now, however, they have no excuse for their sin. He who hates me hates my Father as well. If I had not done among them what no one else did, they would not be guilty of sin. But now they have seen these miracles, and yet they have hated both me and my Father. But this is to fulfill what is written in their Law: "They hated me without reason." When the Counselor comes, whom I will send to you from the Father, the Spirit of truth who goes out from the Father, he will testify about me. And **you also must testify**, for you have been with me from the begin-ning. (John 15:18-27)

Called to be *Witnesses*

Jesus stated that the knowledge we need so we won't go astray is that **we will be persecuted and we must testify about Jesus**. We have all been called to be *witnesses* for the Lord in this dark, sin-cursed age (Acts 1:8). This is how the first-century Christians were, according to the book of Acts.

When I started witnessing (or testifying) about Jesus to others, I simply gave people the word of God. Sometimes I was asked a question I could not answer. I would tell them, "I'll get back with you on that." That gave me a chance to search for an answer in the Bible. After awhile, your ability to fluently witness will become more and more polished as you continue to read and study God's word. **Remember, people are going to Hell all around us and desperately need to know the truth about salvation.**

An excellent way to spread God's eternal truths to others is by having a personal tract ministry, but be sure to use only Biblically sound literature—literature that clearly tells one he must repent (turn from sin) to be saved from Hell. Moreover, don't distribute literature that teaches or implies the lie of eternal security, even if it is free. Our ministry makes available an excellent and very popular dual-colored salvation tract with the vitals about salvation, as well as Heaven and Hell. We also have an important article on tract evangelism that will give you many ideas about using salvation literature. It can be viewed at www.evangelical outreach.org/tracts.htm or obtained from our ministry.

The true gospel, which we are to spread, includes the following truth:

By this gospel you are saved, **if you hold firmly to the word I preached to you. Otherwise, you have believed in vain.** (1 Cor 15:2)

Old Friends

If you are like many, when you first came to the Lord, all your friends are ungodly. In fact, some new converts don't even know a single Christian. But now that you are a follower of Jesus, at least some if not all of these old friends won't like your new priorities. In fact, some might even try to get you to sin or snare you somehow with wickedness. They want you back the way you were when you readily sinned as they still do. Scripture states:

> ... do not share in the sins of others. **Keep yourself pure**. (1 Tim 5:22)

Sin can make a holy person unholy and a pure person impure and no longer fit to enter heaven. It can bring a true Christian to his spiritual death (Rom. 8:13; James 1:14,15 cf. Lk. 15:24,32; etc.). Hence, after you tell your old friends your stand for God, if they want to continue in their sin, don't hang out with them anymore. To continue to spend time and go places with such people will open you to spiritual dangers that would never exist otherwise:

> Do not be misled: "**Bad company corrupts good character**." (1 Cor 15:33)

Remember, your old unsaved friends are in darkness and spiritual death. They do not think or react like you. They are also on the road to Hell, even though they don't know it.

One of the shocking (and vital) truths I learned in the Bible is that Christians are to *avoid* certain people, places and things. Remember also if Eve would never have gone near that tree with the forbidden fruit she would have never been tempted, which led to her sin and leading Adam into sin also. So avoid places of temptation like swimming pools, beaches, discos, Las Vegas, etc. It is also important to dress modestly so you won't cause another to sin (1 Tim. 2:9). Remember also Rom. 12:2:

> **Do not conform any longer to the pattern of this world**, but be transformed by the renewing of your mind. Then you will be able to test and approve what God's will is—his good, pleasing and perfect will.

> **Do not be yoked together with unbelievers.** For what do righteousness and wickedness have in common? Or what fellowship can light have with darkness? What harmony is there between Christ and Belial? What does a believer have in common with an unbeliever? What agreement is there between the temple of God and idols? For we are the temple of the living God. As God has said: "I will live

with them and walk among them, and I will be their God, and they will be my people." **"Therefore come out from them and be separate," says the Lord. "Touch no unclean thing, and I will receive you. I will be a Father to you, and you will be my sons and daughters," says the Lord Almighty.** (2 Cor 6:14-18)

Keep a Clear Conscience

One of the striking truths about Paul's strong and faithful walk with God is shown in the following Scripture:

... there will be a resurrection of both the righteous and the wicked. So **I strive always to keep my conscience clear before God and man.** (Acts 24:15,16)

The importance of this is also expressed as a safeguard against shipwrecking your faith:

Holding on to faith and a good conscience. Some have rejected these and so have shipwrecked their faith. Among them are Hymenaeus and Alexander, whom I have handed over to Satan to be taught not to blaspheme. (1 Tim 1:19,20)

Paul knew the same horrible thing that happened to Hymenaeus and Alexander could also happen to his faithful co-laborer, Timothy. Hence, he gave him these vital responsibilities, which would prevent the loss of his salvation. For us to enter the kingdom of God we will have to endure to the end to be saved (Mt. 10:22). See also Hebrews 3:14 and Rev. 2:10,11. Follow Paul's example and advice to Timothy about keeping a clear conscience. This is also one of the reasons you need to be water baptized by immersion now that you have become a Christian (1 Pet. 3:21). Any true Christian can water baptize you and it doesn't have to be done in a church building.

False Teachers and False Prophets

All new Christians are hungry for God's truth. Oftentimes they can never get enough of His precious word. This is clear evidence of God's saving grace in one's life. But with this hunger for God's truth a new danger is opened up—false teachers! One of the great dangers at the end of our age especially is *religious deception*. There are false teachers around us. Examples are Calvinists, Jehovah's Witnesses, Mormons, Catholics, Muslims, the Church of Christ, "Jesus Only" people and Seventh Day Adventists. These people can be very friendly and zealous, but they are spreading deadly false doctrines, especially about salvation and Jesus himself. See Matt. 7:15.

Beyond them there are also many more false teachers on religious TV and radio, as well as authors of books, articles and tracts, which are not readily known as false teachers. These would especially include **the eternal security teachers and people compromising with the Catholic church**. (Eternal security is, for the most part, an unrecognized rampant heresy in our dark day.) Without writing a mini book on why these people are so dangerous, suffice it to say they dangerously downplay sin in the life of a Christian and de-emphasize the importance of bringing forth good fruit. **Because of eternal security teachers, multitudes are on the road to hell but think they are on the road to heaven. Consequently, their false doctrine needs to be exposed and refuted, not supported. To support such ministries and local congregations will cause you to share in their wicked work.** (For an exhaustive presentation of this teaching with Scriptural refutation, please see our 801 page book entitled, *The Believer's Conditional Security*.) **Don't just trust what you hear someone teach, even if they are a popular teacher over TV, radio or from a pulpit in a local church. Verify and test everything with the Bible, including miracles. You might be surprised to know that both God and the devil can perform miracles. See our important article on this at www. evangelicaloutreach.org/miracles.htm or obtain it from our ministry.**

Churches or *Death Traps?*

Hand in hand with the danger of false teachers can be *going to church*. **Strangely, many churches are spiritual death traps**. Most often the pastor and elder board are apostate themselves and therefore cannot offer sound doctrine and true godly leadership. Such congregational leaders will lull a new convert into lukewarmness and worldliness as they take money from them! This would also include any congregation that would think one can commit "occasional" acts of adultery and murder, like King David did, and still remain saved. If the Christian doesn't flee from such an environment he will often die spiritually because of such a church. It is better and safer to witness to those going to such a local church **after you leave it**. The Christian of our day might have to gather with just a few other true believers in a home where they can worship and seek God together, since a sound congregation is *hard* to find.

Finally, oftentimes the so-called spiritual leaders themselves and the other people in a modern-day church often *hurt* others, especially new converts. For the spiritual health and well being of the Christian, he must forgive others so his sins can likewise be forgiven (Mt. 6:14,15).

Music

Godly music will definitely prove to be a tremendous blessing to the saint. On the other hand, secular music in the form of rock 'n roll, country, oldies, etc. will adversely affect you spiritually. Hence, all music which is not spiritually edifying is potentially dangerous and should be avoided. Again, don't listen to such music at all. I remember hearing a testimony of a woman who fell away from the Lord for a time, which all began because she started listening to country music. Also, remember that just because music might be religious doesn't mean it is doctrinally sound. **Many dangerous anti-scriptural concepts are conveyed in so-called "gospel" music! You should examine the words of a song as you would a teaching—checking it with the Scriptures.**

TV

Perhaps the greatest tool the devil has in the early part of the twenty-first century is television, which can be magnetizing. The sights and sounds can stay with a person long after the show is over. The Bible says:

> For to be carnally minded *is* **death**; but to be spiritually minded *is* **life and peace.** (Rom 8:6)

Since TV shows are produced by ungodly people to draw ungodly people, much harm can come to the Christian through such, besides it being a waste of precious time which could be used to serve God. Even religious TV is far from being beneficial to the viewer with all those false teachers on there, as already mentioned.

The Bible is Final Authority

Another vitally important fact a new Christian needs to know is the Bible is final authority. This means if an experience, vision, dream, prophecy, teaching, testimony, sensation, etc. contradicts the written word of God then reject it. It is not God's truth. Furthermore, you won't ever need more than the Bible to accurately learn about salvation and what God wants from you in this life. Some dangerously think you need to supplement the Bible with Sacred Tradition, the Book of Mormon, the Koran, the writings of the ante-Nicene Fathers, etc. The Bible reads:

> All Scripture is God-breathed and is useful for teaching, rebuking, correcting and training in righteousness, so that the man of God may be thoroughly equipped for every good work. (2 Tim 3:16,17)

The man of God is thoroughly equipped for every good work with the Scriptures alone. If someone thinks the Scriptures are not sufficient then he must not be a man of God. Finally, avoid so-called study Bibles with notes. The *notes* in them are often wrong and don't deserve the same space on the page as Scripture.

A Bible Translation

As a new Christian, I was misled into thinking the King James Version of the Bible is the most accurate translation we can read. Consequently, I spent a number of years struggling over this hard to read and misleading Elizabethan English translation. Many words in the KJV are words that readers have never seen before. Hence, they will often just take a guess at their meanings, while many other words seem to be commonly known but in reality have a different meaning from everyday life. All this adds up to frustration and hindrances in understanding God's precious, eternal word. Don't be deceived by KJV Onlyites who say the KJV is not hard to understand. Obtain a reliable, easy to read and understand translation of the Bible like the New American Standard, New International Version or New Revised Standard. In fact, switch off from these three translations for shades of meanings that are not apparent otherwise. Stay in the New Testament to learn especially what Jesus and his apostles taught about salvation. After you read through it perhaps 10 times, then start to learn the Old Testament while you also continue to read the New Testament.

Memorizing Scripture

Memorizing God's eternal word will have benefits throughout your entire Christian life. There are various reasons why this will help to strengthen, guide and encourage you as it also bolsters your faith to face each new day. The devil will try to hinder you from memorizing God's word. Stick with it and your blessings from such will be great:

> How can a young man keep his way pure? By living according to your word. I seek you with all my heart; do not let me stray from your commands. **I have hidden your word in my heart that I might not sin against you.** (Psa 119:9-11)

Your Soul Is Most Precious

Nothing you own now or ever will own can compare with the value of your soul. Therefore, you need to guard it carefully. See Prov. 4:23. Heaven is real, but so is Hell. To enter the kingdom of Heaven and escape Hell there are things you must do for yourself now that you are saved, so that you will stay saved. There is salvation maintenance and effort that needs to be exerted to stay with God. See 2 Peter 1:5-12. Also, notice what the Lord Jesus taught:

> Someone asked him, "Lord, are only a few people going to be saved?" He said to them, **"Make every effort to enter through the narrow door, because many, I tell you, will try to enter and will not be able to."** (Luke 13:23,24)

It is worth any sacrifice to enter God's eternal, paradise kingdom and escape eternal punishment in Hell fire. The road to life is *hard* (Mt. 7:14) and there are *enemies* along the way, besides the devil, so you will have to dress yourself with the whole armor of God and continue in the faith, even through the rough times that will sometimes come:

> "We must go through **many hardships to enter the kingdom of God,**" they said. (Acts 14:22)

You have a glorious future before you that cannot properly be expressed in words. See Rev. 21:4; Phil. 1:21-23; 1 Cor. 2:9; Isa. 35:10; etc.

Keep your eyes on Jesus, your hand to the plow and don't look back. Immerse yourself in the Bible (especially the New Testament at first) and **put into practice what you read**. Jesus described the true Christians (his real spiritual family) as:

> He replied, "My mother and brothers are **those who hear God's word and put it into practice**." (Luke 8:21)

Several good daily prayers are:

> May **the words of my mouth** and the **meditation of my heart** be pleasing in your sight, O LORD, my Rock and my Redeemer. (Psa 19:14)

> **Turn my heart toward your statutes and not toward selfish gain. Turn my eyes away from worthless things**; preserve my life according to your word. (Psa 119:36,37)

> Direct my footsteps according to your word; **let no sin rule over me**. (Psa 119:133)

24

Never Really Saved

In many Christian circles, the phrase, **"He was never really saved to begin with" seems to be overused in an effort to defend the widespread teaching of eternal security.** This is usually cited in conjunction with a religious person, apparently saved (perhaps even for many years), who later turns to adultery, greed, drunkenness and/or some other similar sin or doctrinal heresy which denies his past Christian profession. It has also been used with certain Biblical characters such as the Apostle Judas Iscariot who, behaviorally, had displayed the same similar thing. Though this phrase has some validity based on Matt. 7:21-23, **it doesn't cover all cases.**

Unwittingly, the proponent of eternal security who uses (even **overuses**) this phrase has spent little or no time pondering the life of the Patriarch David and/or meditating on passages like 1 Cor. 6:9,10 and Rev. 21:8. Without question, David started off as an ultra-committed child of God, during which time he was enabled to kill Goliath, the enemy warrior, with a stone from his sling shot because he so trusted in his God (1 Sam. 17:50) and even before this, killed a lion and bear (1 Sam. 17:36); yet, years later, after becoming King of Israel, he committed **adultery** and successfully plotted the **murder** of the woman's husband (2 Sam. 11) to prevent their joint sin from being openly known! Furthermore, David **lived a lie** for at least nine months, during which time the child conceived in sin was born, for it wasn't until **after** this point in time that he repented due to Nathan's confrontation!

With all these facts in mind, can one rightly say of David, "He was never really saved to begin with" because he committed the sins of **adul-**

tery and **murder**? Obviously not! Why then does this flawed and Scripturally-inconsistent defense of the present-day **mythical** teaching of eternal security continue to be regularly uttered as an airtight, irrefutable answer by those who have been eye-witnesses of a Bible-defined Christian of our day who died spiritually right before their eternal security eyes? **The answer is obvious—for logically, if there can be found just one example of a saved person who later lost his salvation, then their beloved teaching is nothing more than a false security taught under the banner of grace and the finished work of Christ!**

It must also be cited that, with no exception, ALL the sexually immoral and murderers will not inherit the kingdom of God, according to 1 Cor. 6:9,10 and Rev. 21:8, that is, unless they repent. This former passage reads:

> Do you not know that the wicked will not inherit the kingdom of God? Do not be deceived. Neither the sexually immoral, nor idolaters, nor adulterers, nor male prostitutes, nor homosexuals, nor thieves, nor the greedy, nor drunkards, nor slanderers, nor swindlers will inherit the kingdom of God.

Remember also that we should always interpret the Old Testament in the light of the New Testament. Therefore, David's acts of adultery and murder would certainly have excluded him from the Kingdom of God, if he had not repented, according to the Apostle Paul! To believe otherwise is to reject the Biblical evidence regarding this.

Furthermore, true **grace** teaching is best described in Titus 2:12:

> It teaches us to say "**No**" to ungodliness and worldly passions and to live self-controlled, upright and godly lives in this present age.

Besides David, there are other Biblical examples which shed spiritual light on the phrase, "He/She was never really saved to begin with."
Another example is 1 Tim. 5:14,15 which read:

> So I counsel younger widows to marry, to have children, to manage their homes and to give the enemy no opportunity for slander. Some have in fact already turned away to follow Satan.

Please note that one cannot *turn away to follow Satan* unless he/she was first following someone else! Since there is only one other possibility, the widows Paul wrote of must have been following Jesus before they turned to start to follow Satan! Also, verse 11 declares that these same widows originally had a *dedication to Christ*. Clearly, then, their *dedication to Christ* came to an end or died. Then they started to *follow Satan*. This is the Biblical record—like it or not!

In contrast to Paul, many eternal security proponents of our day, if present then, would have been forced to comment that those same widows were "never really saved to begin with" or forfeit their beloved doctrine! Paul, however, clears this up for all time for those of us that have *ears to hear*.

Another refutation is Jam. 4:4b which reads:

Anyone who chooses to be a friend of the world **becomes** an enemy of God.

Notice how James declares that one can *become* an enemy of God. One is either saved or unsaved; with Jesus or against Him; a child of God or an enemy of God. Now, for one to *become an enemy of God* must imply he was, just before that spiritual condition, a child of God. There is no other spiritual condition to be in! Furthermore, raging fire will consume all the enemies of God (Heb. 10:27)! So if one *becomes* an enemy of God from his former spiritual condition of being saved, then he can't be saved anymore, especially since raging fire will consume him! Also, the argument "once a son, always a son" is refuted by the possibility of a saved person becoming an *enemy of God!* In other words, James cites in condensed form that a Christian can come to love the world and show himself no longer saved. He also described what happened to Demas (2 Tim. 4:10)! This, too, is the answer for those who say, based on the Old Testament, that "Christ is married to the backslider," but fail to say, "I gave faithless Israel her certificate of divorce and sent her away because of all her adulteries," Jer. 3:8!

To cite another similar Scriptural proof which refutes this eternal security answer, please consider the following:

The Parable of the Sower declares there are four different types of people who hear the Word of God. The second type mentioned "believe for a while but in time of testing fall away," Lk. 8:13. In Matt. 13:21, the explanation of this type of person is given:

But since he has no root, he lasts only a short time. When trouble or persecution comes because of the word, he quickly falls away.

This type of person does not continue to live spiritually, though there was once **life** produced by the Word of God and personal faith, as the context shows. Also, the Scriptural meaning of *fall away* in context is **die** as evidenced by the **withered** plants. To *fall away* is equated here with ceasing to *believe*. In review, such people after believing through the Word of God in such a way as to produce life, **ceased believing** (which is likened unto *withering*). **For someone to say of such "They were never really saved to begin with" is to contradict the plain teaching of Jesus Christ!**

Moreover, regarding this same parable, the eternal security teachers are also wrong to say it was "a false faith" that such people had, since it didn't endure. **Friend, how could a false faith produce spiritual life?** Obviously it can't!

Finally, sometimes 1 Jn. 2:19 is misapplied to teach, "He was never really saved to begin with." This verse says:

They went out from us, but they did not really belong to us. For if they had belonged to us, they would have remained with us; but their going showed that none of them belonged to us.

Regarding that passage, please consider the following:

■ If the eternal security interpretation of 1 Jn. 2:19 was correct, then we could never know at this moment if someone was really saved or just a professing Christian, who might not be saved.

■ If the eternal security interpretation of this key verse is correct, then how could there be at least 18 clear, Biblical examples of people and types of people who did indeed experience genuine salvation, then afterwards turned away from Christ to the point where they experienced spiritual death? This too would be an impossibility! Therefore, by allowing the immediate context of 1 Jn. 2:19 and these other Scriptures to interpret this Scripture in question, we must reject the eternal security view of this verse. **Without a doubt, Saul, Solomon and the unnamed disciples of Jn. 6:66 were all saved then later turned from God and never came back!** With all of the aforementioned in mind, 1 Jn. 2:19 cannot, therefore, be a spiritual principle as so many use it, but a specific example.

Aren't We Both Saying The Same Thing?

It seems that a somewhat common response from the *never really saved to begin with* crowd is as follows:

> If someone who had professed salvation turns to immorality, we say he was *never really saved*, while you say he *lost* his salvation. **What difference does it make, since we are both in agreement that such is *on the road to hell and needs salvation?***

The answer is twofold and very simple:

1. The *never really saved to begin with* crowd is not consistent with all who turn to immorality. **Sometimes they say such a person continues to remain saved, as they do with King David or the unnamed man of 1 Cor. 5:1-5, even though they turned to wickedness.**

2. Such a response about a person who turns to immorality *never being saved* is not always Biblical. **There are nearly three dozen examples of saved people, named and unnamed in the New Testament that could or did turn away and not even once do the following Scriptures even infer they *were never saved to begin with* because they did turn away. If it did say such in God's word, there would be a contradiction, for King David turned away to immorality and he was clearly saved *before* that point in time.**
    Also, remember Jesus told the five foolish virgins that let their lamps burn out, *I don't know you* (Mt. 25:12), not *I never knew you*. They were previously saved, but were no longer at that point. Their lamps had gone out. Jesus spoke similarly on two other occasions (Lk. 13:25,27).

Possible Spiritual Tragedies Between
Initial and Final Salvation:

(Note: None of the following were labeled *never saved* because they went back)
Don't be deceived! According to Scripture, it is possible for a Christian to:

- drift away (Heb. 2:1)
- wander away (Mt. 18:12,13)
- wander away from the faith (1 Tim. 6:10,21)
- wander away and destroy the faith of others (2 Tim. 2:18)
- lose your saltiness (Lk. 14:34,35)
- fall away (Mt. 11:6; Mk. 14:27,29)
- fall away from grace (Gal. 5:4)
- stop believing and fall away in time of testing (Lk. 8:13)
- turn away from the faith (Mt. 24:10)
- wander away from a pure heart, a good conscience and a sincere faith and turn to meaningless talk (1 Tim. 1:5,6)
- turn back and no longer follow Jesus (Jn. 6:66)
- desert God and turn to a different gospel (Gal. 1:6)
- have his faith shipwrecked (1 Tim. 1:19)
- leave the straight way and follow the way of Balaam (2 Pet. 2:15)
- be like a branch that is thrown away and withers (Jn. 15:6)
- go astray (Jn. 16:1)
- turn away to follow Satan (1 Tim. 5:15)
- depart from the faith (1 Tim. 4:1).
- turn his ears away from the truth and turn aside to myths (2 Tim. 4:4)
- acquire a sinful, unbelieving heart that turns away from the living God (Heb. 3:12)
- fall away to the point where you can't be renewed by repentance (Heb. 6:6)
- turn away from him who warns us from heaven (Heb. 12:25)
- become lukewarm and get spit out of the body of Christ (Rev. 3:15,16)
- not remain faithful and be hurt by the second death (Rev. 2:10,11)
- have God take away your share in the tree of life and in the holy city (Rev. 22:19)
- be carried away by the error of lawless men and fall from your secure position (2 Pet. 3:17)
- be carried away by all kinds of strange teachings (Heb. 13:9)
- return to sin as a dog to its vomit and a washed sow to the mud (2 Pet. 2:20-22)
- become a violent drunkard and be assigned a place with the unbelievers (Lk. 12:45,46)
- get cut off as a branch from an olive tree for not continuing in faith (Rom. 11:19-23)
- not to continue in the teaching of Christ and be without God (2 Jn 9)
- do nothing with his talent and be thrown outside where there is weeping and gnashing of teeth (Mt. 25:24-30)
- not have the truth remain in him and be without the Son and the Father (1 Jn. 2:24,25)
- soil his spiritual clothing and not be worthy to walk with Jesus (Rev 3:4,5)
- not hold firmly to the gospel and therefore to have believed in vain (1Cor. 15:2)

25

Dave Hunt's Dangerous Misrepresentation Of Arminius

In Dave Hunt's book, *What Love Is This?* (published in 2002), he shockingly presents James (or Jacob) Arminius as someone who taught very similarly to Dave Hunt himself, regarding the subject of eternal security! If this gross misrepresentation was done innocently or intention-ally, only God and Hunt know at this time. (It does appear that Hunt could have been deceived by Laurence Vance, who wrote an earlier book very similar to Hunt's entitled, *The Other Side Of Calvinism*. Unfortunately for Hunt's research reputation and the success of his book, he appears to have ignored the context of what James Arminius wrote about eternal security, as will be proven later in this chapter, and seemingly just relied upon Vance, whom he quotes extensively.)

Furthermore, it appears that Hunt is making a strong appeal to the unlearned and misinformed Arminians of our day to push his new book, which is opposed to the first four points of Calvinism, but also openly declares Hunt's license for immorality known as *eternal security*. Hunt's appeal for the Arminians to support his deceptive book, **which will spread eternal security**, seems obvious after he gave the following compli-ments about Arminius:

... James Arminius was actually biblical in his beliefs ... (p. 76).

He stood uncompromisingly for sound doctrine and believed in the infallibility and inerrancy of the Bible as inspired by God (p. 76).

Arminius was evangelical in the gospel he preached (p. 76).

There are so many evangelical historians who praise Arminius as thoroughly orthodox in his doctrine ... (p. 78).

After all those amazing compliments about Arminius coming from a staunch eternal security teacher, who has both proclaimed and tried to defend this horrible doctrine as included under the Christian *Faith*, **Hunt's dangerous misrepresentation of Arminius** is stated on pp. 76, 77:

He [Arminius] also, with these words, defended himself against the false charge that he taught the doctrine of falling away: "At no period have I asserted 'that believers do finally decline or fall away from faith or salvation.'"

It seems that Hunt (or Vance), whomever it was (or both) that actually misread what Arminius wrote, has lifted this statement entirely out of its context, just like he (they) do to try to make the Scriptures teach eternal security. The entire context of what Hunt quotes (and Vance as well) from Arminius is cited below. The reader might have to review the entire passage twice, to better understand why Arminius wrote that actual sentence.

[Arminius wrote two articles in the context of the following quote. The second one is what is quoted below, which deals with the following: *Is it possible for believers finally to decline and fall away from faith and salvation*. On p. 738 this and another premise are cited. It is only the second one which Arminius deals with in this chapter below. The first statement is: *Faith, that is, justifying faith is not peculiar to the elect*, which is mentioned in passing at the end of his chapter. The underlined part from the following quote is what Hunt (and Vance) has taken out of context to apply to Arminius' view on eternal security. **One more final word: please know that Dr. James Arminius was a very deep and analytical theologian, who carefully considered every word which he commented upon, as you will soon see.**]

The Real James Arminius

From: Jacobus Arminius, *The Works of James Arminius*, trans. James and William Nichols [Baker Book House, 1986], Vol. 1, pp. 741, 742:

II. With regard to the Second Article, **I say, that a distinction ought to be made between *power* and *action*. For it is one thing to de-**

clare, that *"it is possible* for the faithful to fall away from faith and salvation," and it is another to say, that *"they do actually* fall away." This distinction is of such extensive observance, that even antiquity itself was not afraid of affirming, concerning the elect and those who were to be saved, "that it was possible for them *not to be saved;"* and that "the mutability by which it was possible for them *not to be willing to obey God,* was not taken away from them,"—although it was the opinion of the ancients, "that such persons never would in reality be damned."—On this very subject, too, the greater part of our own doctors lay down a difference: For they say, "That it is possible for such persons to fall away, if their nature, which is inclined to lapses and defection, and if the temptations of the world and Satan, be the only circumstances taken into consideration: but that they will not *finally* fall away, because God will bring back to himself his own elect before the end of life." If any one asserts, "that it is not possible for believers, in consideration of their being *elect persons,* finally to fall away from salvation, because God has decreed to save them, "I answer, The decree concerning saving does not take away *the* POSSI- BILITY *of damning,* but it removes *damnation itself.* For "to be actually saved," and "a possibility of not being saved," are two things not contrary to each other, but in perfect agreement.

I therefore add, that in this way I have hither to discriminated these two cases: And at one time **I certainly did say**, with an explana- tion subjoined to it, **"that it was possible for believers *finally* to decline or fall away from faith and salvation."** But at no period have I asserted, "that believers do finally decline or fall away from faith or salvation." This article therefore is ascribed to one who is not its author; and it is another offence against historical veracity.

I subjoin, that there is a vast difference between the enunci- ation of these two sentences: (1.) "It is possible for believers to de- cline from the FAITH;" and (2.) "It is possible for believers to de- cline from SALVATION." For the latter, when rigidly and accurately examined, can scarcely be admitted;—**it being impossible for be- lievers, as long as they remain *believers*, to decline from salvation. Because, were this possible, that power of God would be con- quered which he has determined to employ in saving believers. On the other hand, if believers fall away from the faith and become unbelievers, it is impossible for them to do otherwise than decline from salvation,—that is, provided they still continue unbelievers.** Therefore, whether this hypothesis be granted or not, the enunciation cannot be accurately expressed: For if this hypothesis (their perseverance in faith) be granted, they cannot decline; but if it be not granted, they cannot do otherwise than decline. (2.) But that first enunciation includes no hypothesis; and therefore an answer may be given to it simply, either that it is possible, or that it is impossible. For this cause, the second article ought to be corrected in the following manner: **"It is possible for believers finally to fall away or decline from the faith;"** or rather, **"Some believers finally fall away and decline from the faith." This being granted, the other can be necessarily inferred,—"therefore they also actually decline from salvation."**

Respecting the truth of this [Second] article, I repeat the same observations which I made about the First. For the following expressions are reciprocal to each other, and regular consequences: "Faith is peculiar to the elect," and "Believers do not finally fall away from the faith." In like manner, "Faith is not peculiar to the elect," and "**Some believers finally decline from the faith.**"

If Dave Hunt had only read one sentence before the one he quoted, he would have easily detected his own gross misinterpretation of what Arminius wrote. Here are those sentences together, again with Hunt's quote underlined:

> I therefore add, that in this way I have hither to discriminated these two cases: And at one time **I certainly did say**, with an explanation subjoined to it, **"that it was possible for believers *finally* to decline or fall away from faith and salvation."** But at no period have I asserted, "that believers do finally decline or fall away from faith or salvation."

Dear reader, doesn't your righteous indignation for the truth regarding the soundness of Arminius' doctrines and reputation flare up after reading just the previous sentence to the one Hunt (and Vance) lifted out of its context? So why did Arminius state the part quoted by Hunt, which has been misused? Because he (Arminius) believed the following:

> **... it being impossible for believers, as long as they remain *believers*, to decline from salvation.**

But shortly after that, he also clarified this with:

> **On the other hand, if believers fall away from the faith and become unbelievers, it is impossible for them to do otherwise than decline from salvation,—that is, provided they still continue unbelievers.**

That is crystal clear as to the real view of James Arminius, but **there is even more evidence that will help clarify this whole issue. Please note what else Arminius wrote on this same subject:**

> He punishes according to the rule revealed in the Law, by which it is said: **"If thou shalt eat, thou shalt die." [Gen. ii. 17.]**[1]

> For just as any one may be unwilling to be built thereon, so may the same man, if he has begun to be built, fall away, resisting the continuation and confirmation of that building. But **it is not probable that Christ wished to signify by those words that believers cannot fall away from the faith,** because that seems useless. For, since it is necessary for them to have their stability in the rock, and therefore always to rest and lie upon the rock, **they will be more slothful in their care to adhere firmly to the rock in temptations, if they be taught that they cannot fall away from the rock.**[2]

> As regards the opinions of the Fathers, you doubtless know that **almost all antiquity is of that judgment, that believers may fall away and perish.**[3]

> If you affirm that it is here said respecting all who are born of God, that they sin not, and that the seed of God remains in them, I shall take the word "remains" as signifying indwelling, but not the continuation of indwelling. But, **so long as the seed of God is in him, he sins not unto death; yet, by degrees, through his own fault and negligence, that seed may be taken away out of his heart; and so that second communication may perish, just as his first creation in the image**

---

1   Jacobus Arminius, *The Works of James Arminius*, trans. James and William Nichols [Baker Book House, 1986], Vol. 3, p. 195.

2   ibid., p. 455.

3   ibid., p. 455.

of God has died away. But this argument, I allow, is the strongest of all which can be adduced to this purpose.[4]

As to the sixth reason: As long as the members continue in Christ like branches in the vine, so long can they not die away; the life-giving power of Christ, to wit, dwelling in them. **But if they have not borne fruit, then they shall be cut off. (John xv. 2.) But it may happen that the branches bear no fruit, even when grafted into the vine, not by the fault of the root, or of the vine, but of the branches themselves.**[5]

No one, however, exists in Christ except by faith in Christ, which is a necessary means of our union with Christ. **But, if it happens that any one falls away from the faith, he falls away from that union, and consequently from the favour of God wherewith He before embraced him in Christ**. Whence also it is apparent that there is in this solution a begging of the question. For it is inquired "whether believers can fall away from the first grace," that is, "from the favour of God wherewith He embraces them in Christ." It is certain they cannot while they remain faithful, because just so long are they in Christ. **But if they fall away from faith, they fall away also from that first grace.**[6]

The example of David proves nothing. For, even if it be granted that David after commission of adultery and murder had not lost the Holy Spirit, it does not thence follow that He cannot be lost. For a man may sin still more grievously, and on this account lose the Holy Spirit. **But what if I shall say that David did lose the Holy Spirit, after he had committed adultery and murder?** You will reply that it appears from Psalm li. that the matter stands otherwise. **I respond that that Psalm was sung by David after that, having been admonished by Nathan, he had repented of those crimes; but that God, at that time, upon the preaching of Nathan, restored the Holy Spirit to David.**[7]

---

4   ibid., p. 457.
5   ibid, p. 457.
6   ibid., pp. 460, 461.
7   ibid., p. 463.

If David had died in the very moment in which he had sinned against Uriah by adultery and murder, he would have been condemned to death eternal.[8]

Neither has that which AFFIRMS the contrary ever been reckoned as an heretical opinion; nay, **that which affirms it possible for believers to fall away from the faith, has always had more supporters in the church of Christ, than that which denies its possibility or its actually occurring.**[9]

Dave Hunt, We Demand A Public Retraction

Dave Hunt, we demand a public retraction of your misrepresentation of Arminius' teaching of the believer's security which you have stated in your book. If you innocently made this grievous error, please make it right by going public with your mistake now. Had you and James Arminius been contemporaries, he would have refuted your teaching on eternal security as he did others who were also false teachers.

You also cited, in part, what his immediate followers (those who wrote the so-called *Remonstrant Opinions*, which demolish the various lies of Calvinism) declared under section IV:

3. True believers can fall from true faith and can fall into such sins as cannot be consistent with true and justifying faith; not only is it possible for this to happen, but it even happens frequently.

4. True believers are able to fall through their own fault into shameful and atrocious deeds, to persevere and to die in them; and therefore finally to fall and to perish.

Dave, these statements clearly refute your own personal view too. **Those were true Arminians, not the so-called (counterfeit) Arminians of our dark hour that reject the first four points, but still teach eternal security like you. Dave, you are not an Arminian**, even though you correctly reject the first four points of the Calvinistic TULIP.

---

8   ibid., Vol. 2, p. 725.
9   ibid.

Dave Hunt's License For Immorality

Dear reader, concisely stated, Dave Hunt's book chews up and spits out the lying teachings of Calvinism on the first four points, but also misstated Arminius on eternal security and tries to make a distinction between eternal security and the Calvinistic *Perseverance of the Saints.* **One must also question Hunt as to just how much real difference exists between the two being a license for immorality taught under the banner of grace, just like Jude stated all Christians are to** *contend* **against (Jude 3, 4).** Please notice that Hunt has taught the following about the sexually immoral man of 1 Cor. 5:

> The man who had "his father's wife"—a terrible sin—**didn't lose his salvation thereby** ....

That unnamed man, who was committing sexual sin which even pagans didn't do (1 Cor. 5:1), was a Christian, according to author/ teacher Dave Hunt. Hence, Hunt (and Vance) thinks there are Christian adulterers, who don't *lose* **their salvation. This is just like the Calvinists who declare the same kind of lie about the elect, who stray into grievous sin (with David being an example) when in adultery and murder. (Detailed answers from the Bible, with documentation, are found in my book,** *The Believer's Conditional Security.***) No more needs to be said about the so-called differences which exist between Hunt's eternal security and the Calvinistic perseverance of the saints.** These are nothing but surface differences. It's the same old lie the devil used on Eve in the garden, that is, sin won't bring spiritual death.

Again, both Hunt and the Calvinists are in perfect agreement about the saved never dying spiritually (losing their salvation) because of their sins. Because of this, both are essentially the same and must be resisted and boldly refuted by all God fearing Christians. **Their false teachings about the believer's security have totally changed the image of what a real Christian is into the possibility that allows for gross wickedness in the life of one of the** *saints.* **Apparently, they don't realize their doctrine is a contradiction to the meaning of the word** *saint,* **which actually means** *holy one.* **Because of the teaching of eternal security, which Hunt is now again promoting in his book primarily against the first four points of Calvinism, this deadly lie will undoubtedly spread into misinformed Arminian circles. As a five point Arminian, I flatly reject Hunt's book,** *What Love Is This?* **as a book to be used to oppose**

the various lies of Calvinism. His tome is laced with spiritual poison and misinformation by teaching eternal security, misrepresenting Arminius and trying to create a difference between Calvinism's fifth point and eternal security. Reading Hunt's book is like going into a restaurant and eating some good food and some poisoned. I fear for all the people who will think Hunt is sound about his objections to the first four points of Calvinism and will also think he must additionally be right about eternal security.

I can personally testify to the danger of books, like Hunt's, which are sometimes partly true, but also laced with the lie of eternal security. When I was a baby Christian, I read a book refuting the teachings of the Jehovah's witnesses, but which also slipped into it the poisonous teaching of eternal security. I got deceived by this author and for a short time believed in the teaching of eternal security myself! This was before I read through the entire New Testament for myself and noticed the many Scriptures proving the believer's security is conditional. For Arminians to circulate Hunt's book to Christians will open these people up to the spiritual deception of eternal security, which leads to sin, ignorance of the Scriptures, lukewarmness, fruitlessness, etc.

The Believer's Conditional Security

For a much more detailed expose of Dave Hunt's unscriptural teachings on eternal security (with refutation), as well as an open letter from 1996, challenging him to a public debate on this doctrine, please consult our never refuted 801 page book, *The Believer's Conditional Security*. This book has gone around the world and into many seminary libraries. It has been used by God to change numerous eternal security people from the darkness of their doctrine into God-fearing, holy people drawing near to God, as the early Christians were. It is available through our ministry for $19.50 (softback or CD) or $29.50 (hardback), as is other important literature on this subject and others. Send your check into Evangelical Outreach, Box 265, Washington, PA 15301. If ordering outside the USA, add $10.00 for shipping and send an international money order or US dollars. This book, as well as other materials, can be ordered over the internet by coming to our web site www.evangelicaloutreach.org. It is the most exhaustive and comprehensive refutation of eternal security ever written. GOD BLESS YOU.

26

The Perseverance Of The Saints Version Of Eternal Security

If one is acquainted with the various ways eternal security is presented, he will notice there are two versions of this false doctrine. The version that the Calvinists embrace is called the *Perseverance of the Saints.* **Because of the way they most often present it, many who know eternal security is not a Christian teaching are sometimes not so aggressive and outspoken on this particular version as they are the other one, which some call** *antinomianism.* Calvinism's most common presentation has also apparently misled some (who rightly reject eternal security) to give web site links and verbal endorsements of so-called *great* preachers of the past like Spurgeon, Whitefield, Edwards, etc.

Dear reader, please know that Calvinism is a total perversion of *grace,* **how one gets saved, God's sovereignty, etc.** But specifically related to eternal security, the fifth point of Calvinism (the perseverance of the saints) **dangerously downplays the seriousness of sin in the life of a believer** (as the other version also does.) Besides that, the Calvinistic rendering of eternal security is **the most deceitful and inconsistent version of the two.** (The other version is consistently a *license for immorality*, while this one seems to be *not so bad* at times.)

Again, the reason for this confusion is probably the way eternal security is **most often** taught by the Calvinists, that is, if a professing believer turns away from following the Lord to immorality he was *never really saved to begin with* and *a true Christian can never permanently fall away.* **Hence, for the Calvinist, the real issue is true or false conversion and not if a true Christian can lose his salvation or not, since they flatly reject that possibility.** (This is why Calvinist John MacArthur will ludicrously say those of Heb. 6:4-6 were never saved, being forced to declare this because they did clearly *fall away* and could not be renewed again through repentance. He would similarly say the ones of Luke 8:13 only had a *spurious faith*.) If you read the first sentence in this paragraph carefully you should have noticed the words *most often*. **Again, please know that the Calvinists don't teach eternal security *consistently*.**

Let me cite a personal witnessing experience I had with a man who seemingly embraced this view, at least in part. We were talking about eternal security and he dogmatically insisted that it was not a license for immorality. He went on to say if one turns from the Lord he was *never saved*. Then approximately two weeks later the same man told me that **the head deacon in his own Baptist church announced that he has been having an adulterous affair with another woman and was going to divorce his wife for her.** Then he said that **this man is still going to heaven**, but he is going to have his rewards burn up! I reminded him what he said just two weeks before to show him he was *not consistent* and then added that he thinks there are *two types of adulterers*—one type being a Christian bound for heaven and the other being an unsaved person. In contrast, the Bible speaks of only **one type of *adulterer*, who is always unsaved** (1 Cor. 6:9,10; Rev. 21:8; etc.)! **This is exactly what Calvinism is like.**

Calvinists will talk about people professing to believe on Jesus turning to immorality that were *never saved*, then turn right around with their false version of saving faith and in their confessions cite King David as an example of an elect person who strayed into grievous sins and for a time remained therein. **Question: How then can you say that one particular person was *never saved* because he turned to adultery, but a different person was and still is saved while he also commits adultery?** As I stated before, they are inconsistent which reflects false teaching. **Furthermore, their explanations reveal a *license for immorality*, just like the other version of eternal security. The implications are clear about David. If he remained saved while in adultery and murder, then any Christian can do the same and likewise remain saved. This is their version of both *grace* and the *gospel*. (Both versions of eternal security reject the Biblical truth that a righteous person can die *spiritually* because of sin.** King David is a clear example of such. See our chapter on this entitled, "The Righteous Can Die Spiritually." Beyond that, Calvinism has gone on record at the synod of Dort to say that *heretics* oppose the teaching of the perseverance of the saints. (They apparently correctly recognize that the Arminians are not teaching the same about *salvation* as they are.)

Also, consider how Calvinists misinform others about **1 Cor. 5:1-5.** Though not blatant, the Calvinist will have to admit that that unnamed man who was committing a type of sexual sin, **which even pagans don't commit, was a Christian while still unrepentant,** just like the other version of eternal security! Hence, again their non-holiness, license for immorality doctrine surfaces its deadly head again. (See our chapter on this entitled, "That The Spirit May Be Saved" proving that man was unsaved while in this sin. Please note that both versions of eternal security rely on the same feeble arguments and misuse the same Scriptures!

Thirdly, the same Calvinist who will speak of *the truly saved enduring unto the end in the way of holiness* **will also teach a license for immorality when giving their faulty understanding of the** *sin unto death.* Calvinist, D. James Kennedy is a clear example of this. He put in print how a man from his congregation started to have an affair with a married woman and suddenly died physically. This same man **remained unrepentant** and was an example of God chastening those *who are truly his own*, according to this Calvinist. (Dave Hunt, the non-Calvinist, teaches the same way with his version of eternal security.) **Question: Where is the** *enduring to the end in holiness* **with such people** *remaining unrepentant* **and still going to heaven after death?** (Here's another example of Calvinism teaching there are *Christians who are adulterers*.) Calvinists similarly teach that a suicide **(an unrepentant self-murderer)** goes to heaven if he was saved before that point.

Fourthly, John MacArthur is a scholarly Calvinist. This same man often says one is *never saved* if he turns away from the Lord, **but that is not all he says.** Note the following as he comments on 1 Cor. 6:9-11 in his own *MacArthur Study Bible:*

> **While believers can and do commit these sins,** they do not characterize them as an unbroken life pattern.

> Some who used to have those patterns of sinful life were falling into those old sins again, and needed reminding that **if they went all the way back to live as they used to,** they were not going to inherit eternal salvation, because it would indicate that they never were saved.

The eternal security version embraced by Calvinists is again shown to be *inconsistent* **and a** *license for immorality.* Here MacArthur is allowing the following for a Christian (one with saving faith) to be guilty of: sexual immorality, idolatry, adultery, homosexuality, theft, greed, drunkenness, slander and swindling. He adds to that in the second quote, if one does go all the way back and submerges himself in these sins again, that would indicate he was never saved. This leads one to think, "but if Christians stop short ever so slightly from going *all the way back to live as they used to,* then they have been saved even if they commit this list of sins." Though MacArthur hates the carnal Christian teaching given by Ryrie, Stanley and others, here he is teaching almost identically.

For some perplexing reason, some who obediently contend against the counterfeit grace message of eternal security seem to be unacquainted with these deceitful inconsistencies about the Calvinistic version of eternal security. However, after considering the above, it should be clear that **the Calvinistic version of eternal security is not associated with *holiness* as claimed, but is in reality a *license for immorality* just like the other version, but presented in a more deceitful way.**

May God raise up thousands of Christians who will aggressively refute both versions of eternal security for the sake of all the millions of souls that hang in the balance. People in adultery, drunkenness, homosexuality, theft, etc. **need to repent for salvation's sake**, not reward's sake (1 Cor. 6:9,10; Jude 7; Rev. 21:8; etc.), but the eternal security proponents cannot issue this life-giving charge because of their false doctrine. May God also reveal the serious spiritual ramifications of endorsing any Calvinist, even from the past, for their false theology will be woven throughout their writings. To say the least, to certify such grace changers is counterproductive to the kingdom of God and to precious souls.

27

To Enter The Kingdom Of God

Do not be deceived! According to the Bible, to enter the kingdom of God, after initial salvation, **you must**:

■ Go through many hardships (Acts 14:22). ■ Bear good fruit or get thrown into the fire (Jn. 15:6; Mt. 7:19; 3:10). ■ Sow to please the Spirit to reap eternal life (Gal. 6:8). ■ Stand firm through hatred to the end to be saved (Mt. 10:22). ■ Do what is right to be righteous (1 Jn. 3:7,8). ■ By the Spirit put to death the misdeeds of the body to live (Rom. 8:13b). ■ Persist in doing good so that God will give you eternal life (Rom. 2:7). ■ Live holy or the second death will have power over you (Heb. 12:14; Rev. 20:6). ■ Forgive others who sin against you so that your sins can be forgiven (Mt. 6:14,15) and so you won't be accountable once again for your previously forgiven sins (Mt. 18:21-35). ■ Continue to believe on Jesus so that you will live and never die (Jn. 11.25,26). ■ Continue in the teaching of Christ or be without God and eternal life (2 Jn. 9; 1 Jn. 2:24, 25). ■ Hold firmly to the word Paul preached so that your believing is not in vain (1 Cor. 15:2). ■ Keep yourself from idols (1 Jn. 5:21), for all idolaters will be thrown into the lake of fire (Rev. 21:8). ■ Hold firmly till the end the confidence you had at first to share in Christ (Heb. 3:14). ■ Remain faithful to God to the very end so you won't be hurt by the lake of fire (Rev. 2:10, 11 cf. 21:8). ■ Continue to do the will of the Heavenly Father to live forever (Mt. 7:21; 1 Jn. 2:17). ■ Love God for the kingdom of God has been prepared for all who do (1 Cor. 2:9; James 2:5). ■ Hold on to your courage and the hope of which you boast to remain God's house (Heb. 3:6). ■ Hate your life in this world to keep it for eternal life (Jn. 12:25). ■ Keep making an agonizing effort to enter God's kingdom doors for many who try will not enter (Lk.13:23,24). ■ Hold on to faith and a good conscience to prevent shipwrecking your faith (1 Tim. 1:19). ■ Keep yourself pure (1 Tim. 5:22) for the pure in heart will see God (Mt. 5:8). ■ Be an overcomer and faithful follower to escape the lake of fire (Rev. 21:7,8; 2:10,11; 17:14). ■ Have your mind set on what the Spirit desires to live in accord with the Spirit (Rom. 8:5). ■ Continue in God's kindness and faith or get cut off like the Jews (Rom. 11:19-23). ■ Be afraid (and not arrogant) of getting cut off like the Jews (Rom. 11:20). ■ Discipline your body and make it your slave so you won't become disqualified (1 Cor. 9:27). ■ Keep a tight reign on your tongue or your religion is worthless (James 1:26).

Do not be deceived! According to the Bible, to enter the kingdom of God, after initial salvation, **you must not**:

■ Disown Christ or he will disown you (Mt. 10:33). ■ Live according to the sinful nature or you will die spiritually (Rom. 8:13). ■ Reject God by living an unholy life (1 Thess. 4:7,8). ■ Defile your temple or God will destroy you (1 Cor. 3:17). ■ Wander from the truth and remain unrepentant (James 5:19,20). ■ Save your life or you will lose it (Mt. 16:25,26 cf. Mt. 10:28; Rev. 12:11). ■ Become lukewarm and remain lukewarm or you'll get spewed out of the body of Christ (Rev. 3:15,16). ■ Hide your talent so you won't be thrown outside into the darkness where there will be weeping and gnashing of teeth (Mt. 25:24-30). ■ Believe for a while and in time of testing "fall away" (Lk. 8:13 cf. Mt. 13:21) ■ Sow to please the sinful nature for those who do will reap destruction (Gal. 6:8). ■ Live according to the acts of the sinful nature or you will not inherit the kingdom of God (Gal. 5:19-21). ■ Depart from the Father to a life of unrestrained sinning or you will become spiritually dead and lost (Lk. 15:24,32). ■ Become a drunkard, sexually immoral, greedy, a liar, etc., which will cause you to not inherit the kingdom of God but instead end up in the lake of fire (1 Cor. 6:9,10; Gal. 5:19-21; Eph. 5:5-7; Rev. 21:8; 22:15; Mk. 7:20-23). ■ Worship the beast, his image or receive his mark, because all who do will be tormented forever with burning sulfur (Rev. 14:9-12). ■ Take words away from this book of prophecy and have God take from you your share in the tree of life and the holy city (Rev. 22:19). ■ Preach a false gospel and become eternally condemned (Gal. 1:8,9). ■ Soil your spiritual clothes and stay that way or you will be unworthy to be with Jesus (Rev. 3:2-5). ■ Forsake Jesus and God as your first love and remain unrepentant or forfeit your right to the tree of life in the paradise of God (Rev. 2:4-7). ■ Choose to be a friend of this world or you will become an enemy of God (James 4:4). ■ Look back now that you have put your hand to the plow or you won't be fit for God's kingdom (Lk. 9:62). ■ Become impure, shameful or deceitful or you will not enter New Jerusalem (Rev. 21:27). ■ Fall from grace or Christ will be of no benefit to you (Gal. 5:4). ■ Be overcome by evil but instead overcome evil with good (Rom. 12:21). ■ Forsake God or he'll forsake you and you'll perish (2 Chron. 15:2; Isa. 1:28). ■ Turn to crooked ways and get banished with evildoers (Psa. 125:5). ■ Stray from the path of understanding and come to rest with the spiritually dead (Pr. 21:16). ■ Turn from your righteousness and do evil or you will die spiritually (Ezek. 3:20; 18:24; 33:18; Rom. 8:13). ■ Think you are standing firm or you will fall (1 Cor. 10:12 cf. 2 Pet. 1:5-10).

28

A Christian's Future Sins Are Not Automatically Forgiven

The security-in-sin teachers are spiritually dangerous people. Besides all of the other grievous declarations they make, some have also gone so far as to say that a *Christian's future sins are already forgiven,* even before they are committed. **Perhaps, they teach this way in an effort to safeguard their doctrine of eternal security while they continue to tickle ears. I have heard at least one state that** *if* **it was possible for a Christian to lose his salvation, it could only occur through sin.** Hence, by removing (in their minds) the only danger to eternal security, they have erected an imagined indestructible shield for its protection. (Unfortunately, like many other Scriptural issues, the eternal security teachers are oblivious to the two other ways a Christian can lose his salvation besides through sin: [1] Denying Jesus through persecution and [2] Accepting a wrong plan of salvation. See chapter 12 in our 801 page book, *The Believer's Conditional Security* for a detailed explanation.)

Here are two specific examples of what we are dangerously being taught from eternal security teachers **Charles Stanley** and **David Jeremiah** respectively:

> **No matter what you do as a child of God, you are forgiven.** You say, "Murder?" **Forgiven.** "Stealing?" **Forgiven.** "Adultery?" **Forgiven.** "Worshiping Idols?" **Forgiven.**[1]

---

[1]   Charles Stanley, "Continuing Sin," Tape #4, MC213.

Do you realize that when God forgives you, he forgives your past, **your present and your future sin?** Some people struggle with that terribly. They think that God only forgives them of all the sin they committed until they were converted. I had a lady tell me one day, she said, "You know, I know my sins were forgiven when I accepted Christ, but I've done a lot of other sin. How am I forgiven for that?" Well, **you were already forgiven.**[2]

If you are a Christian, try to put yourself in their shoes thinking that your future sins are already forgiven before you commit them. If you accepted that premise, then **your spiritual guard is not only down it is** *gone.* **You won't ever need to guard against personal sin and its defiling abilities since you are** *already forgiven.* This would mean you will always remain spiritually pure, just as you were the day you were saved, **even if you would turn to sexual immorality, drunkenness, theft, idolatry, lying, murder, etc.** You would never have to confess those sins to God that you committed after conversion, repent of them, forgive others who sinned against you, etc. to be purified, forgiven and cleansed, since you were never contaminated by any sin after conversion. In contrast, the *spiritual danger* of failing to do these is clear to anyone who has read through the New Testament with spiritual ears to hear and eyes to see, yet is seemingly hidden from the security-in-sin teachers themselves.

Let me cite some of the reasons why Christians reject the above deplorable teaching as taught by Charles Stanley, David Jeremiah and many others.

The Scriptural Evidence

Please notice what Jesus said to the Christians, after his infinite death on the cross for every person's sins:

Yet you have **a few people** in Sardis who **have not soiled their clothes.** They will walk with me, dressed in white, for they are worthy. (Rev 3:4)

---

[2] David Jeremiah, "When holy wedlock turns to holy deadlock," May 26, 2003.

Comment: All the other people in the church at Sardis did *soil* their spiritual clothes and were no longer *worthy* to walk with Jesus dressed in white. How did the majority, who were previously saved, get *soiled?* The answer is clear when you realize that **sin can defile a Christian and even bring him to his spiritual death.** That is why we have the following Scripture (among others):

> ... Do not share in the sins of others. **Keep yourself pure**. (1 Tim 5:22)

Paul believed Timothy could become spiritually defiled again through sin and consequently told Timothy to keep himself pure. That would be meaningless, if Timothy would turn to sin and automatically be pre-forgiven. Paul (and others) were repeatedly teaching like this, even to the point of telling Christians they could *die* spiritually through sin and *not inherit the kingdom of God*:

> For if you live according to the sinful nature, **you will die**; but if by the Spirit you put to death the misdeeds of the body, you will live (Rom 8:13)

> but each one is tempted when, by his own evil desire, he is dragged away and enticed. Then, after desire has conceived, it gives birth to sin; and sin, when it is full-grown, **gives birth to death. Don't be deceived, my dear brothers.** (James 1:14-16)

> The acts of the sinful nature are obvious: sexual immorality, impurity and debauchery; idolatry and witchcraft; hatred, discord, jealousy, fits of rage, selfish ambition, dissensions, factions and envy; drunkenness, orgies, and the like. I warn you, as I did before, that those who live like this **will not inherit the kingdom of God.** (Gal 5:19-21)

At this point, I could stop this chapter, for it has already been proven that sin committed after conversion can defile a Christian, bring him to his spiritual death and cause him not to inherit the kingdom of God. All of that would be impossible if his future sins were already forgiven before they were committed, like these popular savage wolves in sheep's clothing want us all to believe.

What the Bible teaches about *past* sins being forgiven at the point of repentance and a submissive faith in Jesus (Acts 20:21 cf. 26:20) is shown in the following Scripture:

> But if anyone does not have them, he is nearsighted and blind, and has forgotten that **he has been cleansed from his past sins**. (2 Pet 1:9)

That Scripture was written about any person who had been saved, but since has forgotten he was cleansed from *his past sin.* Please note, a Christian at the point of salvation is cleansed from all his sins up to that moment —*his past sins,* according to Peter. Similarly, Paul stated below:

> When you were dead in your sins and in the uncircumcision of your sinful nature, God made you alive with Christ. **He forgave us all our sins,** (Col 2:13)

All our sins were forgiven in a moment's time when we got *born again.* If a Christian is afterwards deceived or yields to the devil's temptations to sin, the following is given as a remedy:

> **If we confess our sins**, he is faithful and just and will forgive us our sins and purify us from all unrighteousness. (1 John 1:9)

The Apostle John put himself in on that Scripture by using the plural pronoun *we.* In other words, if we don't *confess* those sins to God, which are committed after conversion, then we won't be purified from their effects. (Apparently, no person who believes what the security-in-sin teachers proclaim about this will confess his sins to God and renounce them to get purified, since he thinks they are already forgiven.)

> He who conceals his sins does not prosper, but **whoever confesses and renounces them finds mercy.** (Prov 28:13)

There are other indications that a Christian's future sins are not forgiven and that sin can spiritually defile a believer, even though Jesus died for all sins nearly 2000 years ago:

See to it that no one misses the grace of God and that no bitter root grows up to cause trouble and **defile many**. (Heb 12:15)

Since we have these promises, dear friends, let us purify ourselves from everything that **contaminates body and spirit**, perfecting holiness out of reverence for God. (2 Cor 7:1)

Also, notice the following Scripture which shows that the Apostle Paul knew of *some* who wandered away from a *pure heart*. In other words, sin can adversely affect a *pure heart*. This would be impossible if their future sins were already forgiven:

The goal of this command is love, which comes from **a pure heart** and **a good conscience** and **a sincere faith**. Some have wandered away from these and turned to meaningless talk. (1 Tim 1:5,6)

As Christians, we are also to have a certain frame of mind, a certain type of *hope* that will *purify:*

Dear friends, now we are children of God, and what we will be has not yet been made known. But we know that when he appears, we shall be like him, for we shall see him as he is. Everyone who has **this hope in him purifies himself, just as he is pure.** (1 John 3:2,3)

Jesus taught openly that sin can drag any *lustful* person to *hell*:

But I tell you that **anyone** who looks at a woman lustfully has already committed adultery with her in his heart. If your right eye causes you to sin, gouge it out and throw it away. It is better for you to lose one part of your body than for your whole body to be **thrown into hell**. (Mat 5:28,29)

The Lord also stated the stipulation for a Christian to get his sins forgiven, that is, **he must forgive others who sin against him.** Such a teaching would be impossible if his future sins were all automatically forgiven even before they were committed. If that was true then there would be no conditions to get forgiven, unlike what Jesus stated:

For if you forgive men when they sin against you, your heavenly Father will also forgive you. But **if you do not forgive men their sins, your Father will not forgive your sins.** (Mat 6:14,15)

Then the master called the servant in. "You wicked servant," he said, "I canceled all that debt of yours because you begged me to. Shouldn't you have had mercy on your fellow servant just as I had on you?" In anger his master turned him over to the jailers to be tortured, **until he should pay back all he owed.** This is how my heavenly Father will treat each of you **unless you forgive** your brother from your heart. (Mat 18:32-35)

That is not all we read about a Christian's sins getting forgiven. The prayer of faith can bring healing to the body, as well as **forgiveness of sins**:

Is any one of you sick? He should call the elders of the church to pray over him and anoint him with oil in the name of the Lord. And the prayer offered in faith will make the sick person well; the Lord will raise him up. **If he has sinned, he will be forgiven.** (James 5:14,15)

Another deathblow to the lie that a Christian's future sins are already forgiven is the following passage:

If we deliberately keep on sinning after we have received the knowledge of the truth, no sacrifice for sins is left, but only a fearful expectation of judgment and of **raging fire that will consume the enemies of God.** (Heb 10:26, 27)

Clearly, Heb. 10:26,27 is referring to people who had been converted then decided to deliberately *sin* in a certain way. Instead of believing the ear-tickling deadly lies of our day, let's all cleave to the message of the Bible. Among other things it will show us the following, which also would be impossible if a Christian's future sins were already forgiven:

So then, dear friends, since you are looking forward to this, **make every effort to be found spotless, blameless and at peace with him.** (2 Pet 3:14)

Being *found spotless, blameless and at peace with God* **is not automatic. Christians under** *grace* **are to put forth every effort to remain in this condition:**

> **Make every effort** to enter through the narrow door, because many, I tell you, will try to enter and will **not** be able to. (Luke 13:24)

Dear reader, don't let yourself, family or friends be deceived by the eternal security teachers Scriptural distortions. Contend for the faith against their deadly teachings. Souls hang in the balance. God bless you.

29

Is The Calvinism Of Our Day Different Than It Originally Was?

After John Calvin's teachings, the earliest authoritative explanation of Calvinism is what was given at the Synod of Dort in 1618-19. Nearly three decades later, the wording cited at Dort was slightly altered without changing its substance in the Westminster Confession of Faith, finished in December of 1646. Both of these sources of primitive Calvinism reveal that it **was not different back then, than it is today. Calvinism has always allowed for a Christian to be immoral under their warped concepts of** *grace* **and** *salvation.* Below is exactly how Calvinism was originally worded in these two sources respectively in the early to mid 1600's. Both statements were written about the *elect* under their doctrine of the *perseverance of the saints:*

> Although the weakness of the flesh cannot prevail against the power of God, who confirms and preserves **true believers** in a state of grace, yet **converts** are not always so influenced and actuated by the Spirit of God as not in some particular instances **sinfully to deviate** from the guidance of divine grace, so as to be seduced by and **to comply with the lusts of the flesh;** they must, therefore, be consistent in watching and prayer, that they may not be led into temptation. When these are neglected, they are not only liable to be drawn into **great and heinous sins of the flesh, the world, and Satan,** but sometimes by the righteous permission of God actually are drawn into these evils. **This, the lamentable fall of David, Peter, and other saints described in Holy Scripture, demonstrates** (Article 4).

Nevertheless they may, through the temptations of Satan and of the world, the prevalency of corruption remaining in them, and the neglect of the means of their preservation, fall into grievous sins; and for a time continue therein: whereby they incur God's displeasure, and grieve his Holy Spirit; come to be deprived of some measure of their graces and comforts; have their hearts hardened, and their consciences wounded; hurt and scandalize others, and bring temporal judgments upon themselves (Paragraph 3).

If you carefully read the above, it should be apparent that **Calvinism has always allowed for true Christians to** *comply with the lusts of the flesh* **and, therefore, commit** *great and heinous sins of the flesh, the world and Satan.* King David when in adultery and murder, and Peter, who disowned the Lord, are cited as examples. **Collectively, this allows for the true Christian, according to Calvinism, to be** *adulterous, murderous and one who verbally disowns Jesus before men.* This spells out the same devilish *license for immorality* that has been preached through the centuries to our present dark day.

Somehow some have been misinformed into thinking that the Calvinism preached by Spurgeon, Whitefield, Edwards and others of approximately 150 to 250 years ago was different and more sound than the Calvinism of today. Dear reader, don't be deceived. There is no essential difference! Under their version of *grace* and *salvation,* a Christian can be one who is both adulterous and murderous at the same time. This has never changed throughout the centuries.

Calvinism's *Partial* and *Temporary* Falling Away

Many have a less-than-precise understanding of Calvinism. They think Calvinism teaches *if you are saved you won't fall away* or *if you fall away you were never saved.* A more precise way to describe their view about *falling away* is given by one of their own teachers, D. James Kennedy. This is what he wrote:

It is true that Christians can fall into sin; we can partially and temporarily fall away, but not totally and finally fall away.[1]

---

1   Pamphlet entitled, *Can A Christian Fall From Grace,* p. 10.

Hence, **Calvinism does allow the elect (those regenerated) to** fall into heinous sin and *temporarily* **fall away, at which point they still remain saved, even before repentance.** This is how they can teach a license for immorality. Sometimes they might describe this as simply that a Christian can commit *occasional* acts of sin, but not *lifestyle* sin. (They deny a total and final falling away until they unwittingly teach their warped view of *the sin unto death.*) This type of convoluted reasoning has always been part of Calvinism, but seemingly remains undetected by their own advocates.

Going back to the very teachings of John Calvin himself, we see the same deadly misrepresentation of *salvation* as this man, who burned Michael Servetus at the stake with green wood, comments on the following Scripture:

> **But if a righteous man turns from his righteousness and commits sin and does the same detestable things the wicked man does, will he live?** None of the righteous things he has done will be remembered. Because of the unfaithfulness he is guilty of and because of the sins he has committed, **he will die.** (Ezek 18:24)

John Calvin on Ezekiel 18:24

Calvin used 1,305 words in his twisted explanation of that verse to try to preserve the theology he was willing to kill over. Here is part of what he wrote about David when in adultery and murder, as he comments on Ezek. 18:24:

> ... For the example of David shows that **the elect,** although regenerated by God's Spirit, **not only sin to a small extent,** but, as I have said, **plunge into the very lowest abyss.** David became a **perfidious homicide,** and a **traitor to the army of God;** then that wretched king fell into a **series of crimes:** yet he failed in only one thing, and showed that **God's grace was only suffocated within him, and not altogether extinguished** ....

In contrast to Ezek. 18:24, Calvin stated that David didn't *die* spiritually at all, as Ezekiel preached. All that occurred because of his sinful *plunge into the lowest abyss* was that he *suffocated* God's grace, but didn't *altogether extinguish* it. In other words, **David retained his salvation** while living like the devil at the time. Again, this shows that Calvinism has always allowed for the vilest behavior among the *elect.*

Calvinists are unknowingly confused people embracing a chaotic theology. At times they speak of *holiness,* then they are able to turn 180 degrees in the opposite direction and teach that a true Christian can *fall into grievous sins; and for a time continue therein,* citing David and Peter as *(unholy)* examples of the elect. The Calvinism of the past is just as much a false message about *salvation* as it is today.

Perhaps asking the right pointed question(s) will also be helpful to expose the true heart of Calvinism to those you know. Let me recommend the following two: (1) Did David remain saved while in *adultery* and *murder,* before he repented? (2) Can a true Christian stray to that same extreme and likewise *remain saved?* The true Calvinist of our day, just like Spurgeon, Whitefield and Edwards of the past, would be forced to answer yes to both of these questions, in spite of the Scriptural evidence! Remember, they think *once elect always elect* and even the vilest sins can't change that. Calvinism, past and present, needs to be exposed, resisted and refuted not encouraged or spread, especially by those who know *eternal security* is not a Christian teaching. For more information see our chapters entitled, *The Perseverance of the Saints Version of Eternal Security* and *The Righteous Can Die Spiritually.* God bless you.

30

Do All Five Points Of Calvinism Hang Or Fall Together?

It is very common to run into religious people who would identify themselves as four point Calvinists, three point Calvinists on down to one point Calvinists. Such people reject one or more of the five points of Calvinism's TULIP, but always seem to embrace the most deadly of the five—*the perseverance of the saints* (or *eternal security*). How logical is it for such a person who calls himself a *Calvinist* to be less than a five point Calvinist in light of the theology of Calvinism?

Certainly, to the surprise of many, such is an ***inconsistency***, according to one of their chief spokesmen, the deceased Dr. Edwin H. Palmer. Palmer graduated from Harvard, served in the Marines, then received both a Th.B and a Th.D in different Reformed seminaries. He was also an instructor of *Systematic Theology* in a Reformed Seminary. Hence, he is certainly qualified to comment on how the five points of Calvinism are interrelated, since he understood his theology so well. Palmer, referring to the fifth point of Calvinism, said the following:

> **This is strictly a Reformed doctrine and hangs or falls together with the other four points** that we have been discussing. There are, however, Christians today who hold to the perseverance of the saints while at the same time rejecting the other four points. **We believe, however, and will try to show later on, that this is an inconsistency in their thinking.** (*The Five Points of Calvinism*, Moelker Printing Co. [Grand Rapids, Michigan], 1954 ed, p. 59.)

In keeping with his expert opinion of this theology, Palmer went on to write about the perseverance of the saints:

This doctrine also naturally follows from the doctrine of the limited atonement ... (ibid., p. 61).

In other words, if the doctrine of *limited atonement* is true, then so is the perseverance of the saints. But then on the other hand, if limited atonement is untrue, so is eternal security. **The aforementioned two quotes from Palmer are valuable to Christians who know all five points of Calvinism are not from God and especially desire to help free some Calvinists from the theological snare they are trapped in.**

Many Calvinists, who are less than five pointers, correctly reject *limited atonement* because of the Scriptural evidence which powerfully and clearly teaches that Jesus died for every person who ever lived and not just for those who will enter God's kingdom in the end. It is, therefore, *inconsistent* for eternal security proponents to reject limited atonement and still believe in the favorite fifth point—eternal security! Again, this is not my conclusion, but the conclusion of one who knew Calvinism when he was alive, much better than the vast majority does today.

In 1980, the year of Palmer's death, an enlarged edition of this same book was released. In this more recent edition the words were slightly changed from the previous quote, while retaining its essence:

All five points of Calvinism hang or fall together (*The Five Points of Calvinism*, Baker Books [Grand Rapids, Michigan], 1980 enlarged edition, p. 69).

Dear reader, if you know that any of the five points of Calvinism are unscriptural, then the rest are as well. All a Christian has to do, therefore, is to refute any of the five points of Calvinism and by doing so he has destroyed all five points, according to Dr. Palmer himself. But dear Christian, please be assured that people who embrace Calvinism's beloved fifth point won't surrender it easily. They often feel just like Palmer did as reflected in his following statement:

The teaching of "once saved, always saved" is one of the grandest of Biblical teachings (ibid., p. 79).

31

True Or False Conversion Is Not The Big Issue!

Among many who profess to be evangelicals, the big issue regarding how a professing Christian lives is often said to be true or false conversion. In other words, if one who professes to be a Christian then strays into open, blatant immorality *sometimes* it will be mentioned that all he had was a *false conversion* and therefore was *never really saved at all.* [**At other times, the salvation of a person who strays into wickedness is never questioned, as when King David strayed into adultery and murder. This is one of the amazing inconsistencies they are blinded to**.] True or false conversion is their *sometimes-answer* and an eternal security theological loophole to avoid being accurately branded as a *license for immorality* teacher.

The two passages cited (and misused) to exalt true or false conversion into the big issue (when it isn't) are 1 John 2:19 and Mt. 7:23. Let's look at these Scriptures, and their context, in that order.

1 John 2:18-26

The Apostle John wrote the following:

Dear children, this is the last hour; and as you have heard that the antichrist is coming, even now many antichrists have come. This is how we know it is the last hour. They went out from us, but they did not really belong to us. **For if they had belonged to us, they would have remained with us**; but their going showed that none of them belonged to us. But you have an anointing from the Holy One, and all of you know the truth. I do not write to you because you do not know the truth, but because you do know it and because no lie comes from the truth. Who is the liar? **It is the man who denies that Jesus is the Christ. Such a man is the antichrist**—he denies the Father and the Son. No one who denies the Son has the Father; whoever acknowledges the Son has the Father also. **See that what you have heard from the beginning remains in you. If it does, you also will remain in the Son and in the Father. And this is what he promised us—even eternal life.** I am writing these things to you about those who are trying to lead you astray. (1 John 2:18-26)

John is warning Christians about dangerous false teachers whom he calls *antichrists*. Those same antichrists were trying to teach the Christians a spiritually deadly doctrine, which caused John to have godly concern. They were antichrists because they denied Jesus was the Christ (v. 22). [The problem was over *doctrine*, not morality.] The same *antichrists* didn't remain with the apostle John, but left, showing they were also false apostles by not remaining [and teaching as the true apostles did—that Jesus is the Christ].

John wanted his readers to know that **they must *continue* to embrace the true doctrine about Jesus being the Christ *to remain* in the Son and in the Father (v. 24). It was the Christian's responsibility to *continue* to believe this truth about Jesus. Such, according to John, was nothing less than a *salvation* issue, for it deals with *eternal life* (v. 25).**

Mt. 7:20-23

Jesus taught:

Thus, **by their fruit you will recognize them.** Not everyone who says to me, "Lord, Lord," will enter the kingdom of heaven, but **only he who does the will of my Father who is in heaven.** Many will say to me on that day, "Lord, Lord, did we not prophesy in your name, and in your name drive out demons and perform many miracles?" Then I will tell them plainly, "**I never knew you.** Away from me, you **evildoers!**" (Mat 7:20-23)

The Lord here is referring to religious people, who did the same signs and wonders that real Christians did in the Book of Acts, but Jesus said they were *never saved* (v. 23). The eternal security teachers never mention the fact that v. 23 also identifies those same religious people as **continuous-tense evildoers**, as the Greek shows. They were never set free from the slavery of sin. [It is important to remember, the *fruit* by which we can know a person (v. 20) is not their miraculous deeds, but instead their moral life, and those evildoers performing miracles were lacking this evidence.]

The latter part of Mt. 7:21 is not readily known either. That verse reads:

> Not everyone who says to me, "Lord, Lord," will enter the kingdom of heaven, but **only he who does the will of my Father who is in heaven**.

The above verse also proves that it takes a **continuous tense** *doing of God's will*, according to the Greek, to enter God's kingdom. This fact is declared by only some of the eternal security teachers when they are cornered by Christians over their license for sin doctrine.

Among other things, we just learned that 1 John 2:18-26 emphasizes the importance of continuing in certain doctrine for salvation's sake (even among those who have already been saved), while Mt. 7:20-23 magnifies the importance of moral living as the *fruit* of present tense salvation. **Both of these truths are denied by the eternal security teachers who use (or more properly misuse) these same passages to conceal the true identity of their own theology (security-in-sin).**

The Bible has dozens of Scriptures which show there is *evidence of saving grace* and that **the early church knew who was saved and who wasn't.** (See our book, *The Believer's Conditional Security*.) **Hence, if a person who showed evidence of being a Christian turned away from God in the early church, they never thought it was a false conversion.**

Besides all of that, those same people (Calvinists) say election is *secret* and one who might think he is saved could be deceived and only have an *evanescent grace*, according to John Calvin. The Apostle John, who gave us 1 John 2:19, also gave us 1 John 3:10, which says:

> This is how we **know** who **the children of God** are and who **the children of the devil** are: Anyone who does not do what is right is not a child of God; nor is anyone who does not love his brother.

The Lord's apostles taught that one's present tense *behavior* would identify who was a child of God and who was a child of the devil. Since this is what the early Christians believed and openly taught, this is also what we better believe and teach or we are in trouble with God, as well as being a snare for others. The problem for many is, their eternal security theology will not allow them to teach as John did, that is, **our present tense** *behavior* **identifies us as a Christian or non-Christian.**

The Real Issue—*Is He Saved Now?*

The real issue isn't if one was truly saved or not (even though that is important), but instead *is he saved now.* There are over a dozen examples of people in the Bible who once had salvation and afterwards died spiritually and became *lost* again. This is spiritual reality and needs to be the emphasis, for it carries with it the vital warning that the same horrible thing can also happen to any real Christian in our day, if spiritual precautions are not taken. Hence, Christians must be on their much-needed guard to endure and remain faithful to Jesus to the end for their own salvation's sake.

In deadly contrast, all eternal security teachers will do everything they can with their Scripture twisting to convince the real Christian that his salvation cannot be lost under any circumstances, including adultery, drunkenness, murder, etc. As we have said before, all eternal security teachers (also known as *the perseverance of the saints, once saved always saved or the preservation of the saints*) are very dangerous people, though they are usually considered to be great spiritual leaders in our dark day. It is long overdue to set the record straight about these issues and to *contend* steadfastly against these *grace* changers (Jude 3,4) who have led millions to hell by their venomous teachings!

Stop Helping The Enemy!

Please know that to donate to or financially support eternal security congregations or ministries is to help spread this sinister doctrine and to be *partly responsible* for all the harm/evil that will be done through them (2 John 10,11). The same can be said by giving them a web site link or attending their congregations. Take this warning to heart and stop assisting the spread of this poisonous doctrine, which had its origin with the devil.

32

Christians Can Quickly Turn To Another Gospel

Paul wrote to the churches in Galatia, that is, those he founded at Antioch in Pisidia, Lystra, Derbe and Iconium as mentioned in Acts chapters 13 and 14 on his first missionary trip:

Grace and peace to you from God **our Father** and the Lord Jesus Christ, who gave himself for our sins to rescue us from the present evil age, according to the will of our God and Father, to whom be glory for ever and ever. Amen. **I am astonished that you are so quickly deserting the one who called you by the grace of Christ and are turning to a different gospel**—which is really no gospel at all. Evidently **some people** are throwing you into confusion and are **trying to pervert the gospel of Christ**. But **even if we** or **an angel from heaven** should preach a gospel other than the one we preached to you, let him be **eternally condemned**! As we have already said, so now I say again: If **anybody** is preaching to you a **gospel** other than what **you accepted**, let him be **eternally condemned**! Am I now trying to win the approval of men, or of God? Or am I trying to please men? **If I were still trying to please men, I would not be a servant of Christ**. (Gal. 1:1-10)

There is no question that God was their spiritual *Father* (1:3) and that they *accepted* the real gospel when Paul preached it to them (1:9). That is also confirmed in Acts:

The next day he and Barnabas left for Derbe. **They preached the good news in that city and won a large number of disciples**. Then they returned to **Lystra, Iconium and Antioch, strengthening the disciples and encouraging them to remain true to the faith**. "We must go through many hardships to enter the kingdom of God," they said. Paul and Barnabas appointed elders for them in each church and, **with prayer and fasting, committed them to the Lord, in whom they had put their trust**. (Acts 14:20-23)

Without question, Acts 14:20-23 show the recipients of the Book of Galatians were really saved. After they came to salvation, *some people* (1:7) [false teachers] came and preached a false gospel to these Christians and *they were in the process of turning to that false gospel* (1:6), when this epistle was being written. Furthermore, this turning to a false gospel happened *quickly* and *astonished* Paul (1:6). This proves that real Christians can be *fatally deceived* by false teachers.

Verses 8 and 9 magnify the one and only gospel to the zenith of importance by stating that even if Paul, one of God's angels or anyone else would preach a *gospel* that is different than the one Paul preached, then let that person be *eternally condemned.* The TEV renders 1.8 as **condemned to hell! The Bible teaches that one can go to hell just for preaching a false Gospel,** according to these verses. Why is this true? Because such a false teaching can cause a repeat of what was happening to the Galatian Christians. The seriousness of those Galatians believing a false gospel is shown in chapter 5:

Mark my words! I, Paul, tell you that if you let yourselves be circumcised, **Christ will be of no value to you at all**. Again I declare to every man who lets himself be circumcised that he is obligated to obey the whole law. You who are trying to be justified by law have been **alienated from Christ; you have fallen away from grace.** (Gal. 5:2-4)

Regardless how the eternal security teachers would twist the plain meaning of these Scriptures and sometimes say ridiculous things like *you can fall from grace and never be in grace*, we have already seen positive proof Paul was writing to true Christians. The meaning of and danger behind the words *you have fallen away from grace* is revealed in 5:2. That is where Paul wrote, *Christ will be of no value to you at all.* To *fall from grace* means to **not have value from Christ anymore.** For one who is a Christian that can only mean that **he doesn't have salvation anymore, since you can't have salvation without Christ.**

Paul clearly warned of the lethel dangers of preaching *another gospel* and/or believing *another gospel* in this epistle. This is all related to what can happen under *grace* to real Christians and in itself disproves the popular, but heretical, teaching of eternal security.

Furthermore, for people to say that *doctrine is not important* is grossly dangerous, besides being a doctrine itself. (To them their doctrine that *doctrine is not important* is important.) Paul certainly believed doctrine was important, especially if it centers around the *gospel*.

It is amazing how the eternal security teachers distort the word of God to make it fit into their theology instead of shaping their theology around the word of God. If they shaped their theology around the Bible they would have to reject eternal security. Sadly many think that would be too high a price to pay as it would adversely affect their temporal "ministry" and reputation.

An example of distorting Scripture to fit eternal security would be how Dave Hunt deals with Galatians chapter 1. Below is first a question, then Hunt's answers:

Dear TA and Dave, I have read the book of Galatians more than once and each time it puzzles me as to **whether or not Paul is telling them that they are in danger of losing their salvation by turning to another gospel.** I believe there is only one true gospel that can save a person and it's from that gospel that the Galatians are turning. However, **I also believe that the Bible teaches eternal security. So I don't believe they could become lost. Therefore, I can't quite resolve these apparent conflicts.** What do you say?

[TA]: Paul's pretty strong in his condemnation of those who are turning to the law, turning to circumcision in Galatians and he calls that another gospel. But is he indicating that they might not, that they may be losing their faith or turning from the faith or losing their salvation?

[Dave Hunt]: It's not a question of losing your salvation. What Paul is concerned about is, **did you really understand the gospel to begin with?** He says, I stand in doubt of you. He tells them ...

[TA]: Yeah but he says, doesn't he say in chapter 3 **they began with the Spirit.**

[Dave Hunt]: Well, no, he's reasoning with them there. He's not saying that, **that doesn't have to do with their salvation right then**. But that has to do with their living the Christian life. And if you got the Christian life by faith through Christ, then you can't generate this yourself. What you began in the Spirit you can't perfect in the flesh. I think he's arguing that with them. He's already said, I'm crucified with Christ, nevertheless I live yet not I but Christ is living, living in me. But he also in chapter 5, verse 4 for example, says Christ has become of no effect unto you whosoever of you are justified by the law. You are fallen from grace. **Now I don't think he means you can lose your salvation**. What he's saying is, well earlier he says, **I stand in doubt of you. Are you really Christians?**

Dear reader, can you see the *poison* **that is being taught by these eternal security teachers and how if differs from what Scripture really says?**

Isn't it sad that the person who asked the question actually saw its meaning in Scripture—*the danger of losing salvation by turning to another gospel,* but because of their erroneous belief in eternal security that person would not accept what the Bible clearly teaches. It is also unfortunate that that person asked someone like Dave Hunt, who embraces eternal security. (Please know Dave Hunt is no worse than any other eternal security teacher. They are all alike, that is, they *all* distort the Scripture to make it fit their security-in-sin doctrine/theology.)

Also remember that the established religious leaders in Jesus' day were evil and wanted him dead. Should we be surprised that so many in our day, nearly 2,000 years later, are the same or close to it as far as being blind leaders?

Remember also that the above misinterpretation of Gal. 1 is just one example that is dangerously distorted and which may come from any eternal security teacher on this subject.

May God help us all.

33

Backslider, God Wants You Back!

A *backslider* is a person who once had salvation, but has since turned away from the Lord Jesus to the point that he is now spiritually *lost* and *dead* again, just like he was before becoming saved. The Bible is filled with examples of people, named and unnamed, who turned away from God temporarily or permanently. Some returned, like King David and Peter, while others never came back to God, like kings Saul and Solomon.

A common contact that our ministry receives is from the grieving backslider, who wants to come back to God, but isn't sure that he can. Some think they sinned too much and too grievously while others think they committed *eternal sin* and therefore can't get forgiven. There is, perhaps, no more downcast person to communicate with than a repentant person who isn't sure he can come back to God and find forgiveness, though he desperately wants forgiven!

Years ago, when I was pastoring, I knew a person who was previously saved but afterwards fell into sexually immorality. Over the next couple days that man lost nearly 10 pounds and was actually, on occasions, beating his own head against the wall in regret over his sin and foolishness. (He wrongly thought he was doomed to hell with no possible hope of ever getting saved again.) What finally helped this man to see that he could come back to God, in spite of his wicked actions, were the examples of King David and the Apostle Peter. Since God took these men back, why should he not take him too, since he was deeply repentant and resolved to never commit that sin again.

Other examples of grieving backsliders would vary from people crying to simply asking if they could possibly find forgiveness once again. For such people, we often tell them of the teaching of the Lord Jesus in Luke 15:11-32. In our day, we call that teaching the *Parable of the Prodigal*, though it not actually called this in the Bible. The highest authority on the backslider, and how God reacts to a repentant one, taught the following:

Jesus continued: "There was a man who had two sons. The younger one said to his father, 'Father, give me my share of the estate.' So he divided his property between them. Not long after that, the younger son got together all he had, set off for a distant country and there **squandered his wealth in wild living**. After he had spent everything, there was a severe famine in that whole country, and he began to be in need. So he went and hired himself out to a citizen of that country, who sent him to his fields to feed pigs. He longed to fill his stomach with the pods that the pigs were eating, but no one gave him anything. **When he came to his senses**, he said, 'How many of my father's hired men have food to spare, and here I am starving to death! I will set out and go back to my father and say to him: Father, I have sinned against heaven and against you. I am no longer worthy to be called your son; make me like one of your hired men.' So he got up and went to his father. But while he was still a long way off, **his father saw him and was filled with compassion for him; he ran to his son, threw his arms around him and kissed him**. The son said to him, 'Father, I have sinned against heaven and against you. I am no longer worthy to be called your son.' But the father said to his servants, 'Quick! Bring the best robe and put it on him. Put a ring on his finger and sandals on his feet. Bring the fattened calf and kill it. Let's have a feast and celebrate. For this son of mine **was dead and is alive again; he was lost and is found**.' So they began to celebrate. Meanwhile, the older son was in the field. When he came near the house, he heard music and dancing. So he called one of the servants and asked him what was going on. 'Your brother has come,' he replied, 'and your father has killed the fattened calf because he has him back safe and sound.' The older brother became angry and refused to go in. So his father went out and pleaded with him. But he answered his father, 'Look! All these years I've been slaving for you and never disobeyed your orders. Yet you never gave me even a young goat so I could celebrate with my friends. But when this son of yours who has squandered your property with **prostitutes** comes home, you kill the fattened calf for him!' My son, the father said, 'you are always with me, and everything I have is yours. But we had to celebrate and be glad, because this brother of yours **was dead and is alive again; he was lost and is found.**' "

Observations

■　The prodigal repented when he **came to his senses**. This means a person who remains unrepentant and in sin that is dragging him to hell is not in his right spiritual senses. He has been spiritually blinded by something or deceived somehow.

■　The prodigal was able to find forgiveness after he turned from all the wickedness he had been in that held him in spiritual death. Repentance (turning from sin) to serve God is illustrated in this teaching. Though he was in *wild living*, including sexual sin with *prostitutes*, for an unknown period of time—perhaps many years—he still found forgiveness.

■　The prodigal became *alive again* and his *lost* spiritual condition changed upon turning from all those sins and humbly coming back to the Father to serve him. Compare to 1 Thess. 1:9b.

■　The only time in the Bible that we read where **the Father ran** is in this teaching and **it was to welcome the repentant backslider back home.**

■　The Father was so happy to have him back he hugged and *kissed* him as well as *celebrated.*

■　Some Christians who correctly reject the teaching of eternal security wrongly think that no one who ever **falls away** can come back. This is clearly refuted by Jesus' teaching here, as well as other passages (Rom. 11:19-23 and James 5:19,20).

■　This teaching proves that a spiritually *lost* and *dead* person could be a person never saved or one that was once saved.

God Delights to Show Mercy to the Repentant!

The fact that God **delights to show mercy to the repentant** is illustrated in Jesus' teaching, but also candidly declared in the following passage:

Who is a God like you, who pardons sin and forgives the transgression of the remnant of his inheritance? You do not stay angry forever but **delight to show mercy**. You will again have compassion on us;

you will tread our sins underfoot and **hurl all our iniquities into the depths of the sea** (Micah 7:18,19).

Another relevant passage is:

> He who conceals his sins does not prosper, **but whoever confesses and renounces them finds mercy** (Prov 28:13).

Did you notice that the returned prodigal *confessed* his sins and wicked actions to the Father (and not to any man, including a priest). This is the Lord's teaching on this:

> The son said to him, **"Father, I have sinned against heaven and against you**. I am no longer worthy to be called your son" (Luke 15:21).

The Bible also says about those who sin after getting saved:

> If we confess our sins, he is faithful and just and will forgive us our sins and purify us from all unrighteousness (1 John 1:9).

David's prayer as a backslider returning to God and **asking God for forgiveness** shows **the pain and misery**, he and others like him, are in. When the devil is tempting the righteous to sin, he will never accurately portray sin in this manner:

> For the director of music. A psalm of David. When the prophet Nathan came to him after David had committed adultery with Bathsheba. **Have mercy on me, O God, according to your unfailing love; according to your great compassion blot out my transgressions. Wash away all my iniquity and cleanse me from my sin. For I know my transgressions, and my sin is always before me. Against you, you only, have I sinned and done what is evil in your sight**, so that you are proved right when you speak and justified when you judge. Surely I was sinful at birth, sinful from the time my mother conceived me. Surely you desire truth in the inner parts; you teach me wisdom in the inmost place. **Cleanse me with hyssop**, and I will be clean; wash me, **and I will be whiter than snow.** Let me hear joy and gladness; let the bones you have crushed rejoice. Hide

your face from my sins and **blot out all my iniquity. Create in me a pure heart, O God, and renew a steadfast spirit within me. Do not cast me from your presence or take your Holy Spirit from me** (Psa 51:1-11).

Had the prodigal (or David) died physically when in their backslidden condition, they would have gone to *fiery torment*. We can all rejoice that they came back to the Father, but this is **not always the case. God's discipline doesn't always bring the wayward back (Jer. 32:33).** Many turn away and die physically in that lost condition, such as the Apostle Judas Iscariot. Don't be deceived by those who would say that *Judas was never saved.* (Please see our book, *The Believer's Conditional Security*, pages 279-286.)

Similar to the fact that there are two types of *lost* people, as stated earlier, there are also two types of *wicked* people. This is reasonable since the spiritually *lost* are also *wicked* in God's eyes. **But many in our day would wrongly consider the backslidden, who were previously saved, carnal Christians or elect people in grievous sin and not unsaved (wicked) at all. Such has been produced by the pernicious theology of eternal security as embraced by multitudes of religious deceived people. We have noticed that eternal security proponents don't usually repent of their sins until they first learn that there is no such thing as eternal security, once saved always saved or the perseverance of the saints, that is, there is no such thing as security in sin.**

The Backslidden are Wicked

Scripture shows that the backslidden are *wicked*:

For the director of music. Of David the servant of the LORD. An oracle is within my heart concerning the sinfulness of **the wicked**: There is no fear of God before his eyes. For in his own eyes he flatters himself too much to detect or hate his sin. The words of his mouth are wicked and deceitful; **he has ceased to be wise and to do good**. Even on his bed he plots evil; he commits himself to a sinful course and does not reject what is wrong (Psa 36:1-4).

That fact is also a deathblow to the teaching of eternal security because **the *wicked* are always unsaved people on the road to the fiery furnace:**

> **Salvation is far from the wicked**, for they do not seek out your decrees (Psa 119:155).

> This is how it will be at the end of the age. The angels will come and separate the **wicked** from the righteous and **throw them into the fiery furnace, where there will be weeping and gnashing of teeth** (Mat 13:49,50).

Are You Biblically *Wise?*

To be a Biblically *wise* person, one must put into *practice* the word of God and by doing such he is identified as a member of Jesus' spiritual family. Dear reader, take to heart Jesus' teaching on this:

> Therefore everyone who hears these words of mine and **puts them into practice** is like a **wise** man who built his house on the rock. The rain came down, the streams rose, and the winds blew and beat against that house; yet it did not fall, because it had its foundation on the rock. But everyone who hears these words of mine and does not put them into practice is like a **foolish** man who built his house on sand. The rain came down, the streams rose, and the winds blew and beat against that house, and it fell with a great crash (Mt. 7:24-27).

> He replied, "**My mother and brothers are those who hear God's word and put it into practice**" (Luke 8:21).

Getting back to Psalm 36:3, to **cease to be wise and to do good** shows that such a person was once God's child at a prior point in time, but since has lost that spiritual identity and taken on a new identity—*wicked*. **In other words, when one turns to this degree he loses his salvation.** This is taught many other times in the Bible:

> But **those who turn to crooked ways** the LORD will banish **with the evildoers** (Psa 125:5).

But rebels and sinners will both be broken, and **those who forsake the LORD will perish** (Isa 1:28).

Eternal Sin

Jesus was the only one who ever mentioned *eternal sin* and at the same time told us clearly what it is:

But whoever blasphemes against the Holy Spirit will never be forgiven; he is guilty of an **eternal sin**. He said this because **they were saying, "He has an evil spirit"** (Mark 3:29,30).

If you would go back and start reading at Mark 3:22 you will learn more about those who committed such a form of blasphemy. **They were saying that Jesus had a demon and by the power of the devil he was casting them out and performing his miracles.** This is what Jesus identified as eternal sin. It is **not** adultery, murder, disowning Jesus, or any other kind of sin. All of the latter can be forgiven, but not *eternal sin.* **Another sin that can't be forgiven is the mark of the beast, Rev. 14:9-12.** (Eternal sin is apparently the type of sin those mentioned in Heb. 6:4-6 committed and, therefore, they could not be renewed again by repentance.)

So, backslider come home. God wants you back. **It is the devil that is tormenting your mind and trying to make you think you cannot return to God.** Remember also all the good that Peter did after he returned to God from his backslidden condition. **God used him mightily and can do the same with you. Yes, you too can do great things for the kingdom of God, if you have sincerely returned to God from wickedness and will faithfully serve him.** May God use these eternal truths to spiritually enlighten real truth seekers who are in desperate need of knowing this vital material.

34

Are You Sure There Are None That Are Righteous?

This chapter came as the result of obeying the command to contend for the faith against those who change grace into a license for immorality (Jude 3,4). The person I dialoged with was a Baptist minister's wife. While I was talking about the defiling, corrupting and deadly effects of sin for the righteous and mentioning that Paul told Timothy *to keep himself pure* (1 Tim. 5:22) because he knew Timothy could sin and become impure and even die spiritually, she interjected the frequently quoted verse from Romans 3:10 which states that there is no one that is righteous. That verse reads:

As it is written: **There is no one righteous, not even one** ....

Because this verse is so universally known among those who profess salvation and claim to believe the Bible, it is important to examine this carefully. Another Scripture sometimes used for the same cause is Eccl. 7:20 such as what the so-called "great theologian" George Whitefield did against John Wesley in "A Letter from Mr. George Whitefield in 1740 to the Rev. Mr. John Wesley" in answer to Wesley's sermon entitled "Free Grace." Whitefield wrote:

And since the Scriptures declare **that there is not a just man upon earth** (no, not among those of the highest attainments in grace) that doeth good and sinneth not (Eccl. 7:20), **we are sure that this will be the case of all the children of God.**

Actual Named People

To ascertain the meaning of any Scripture we must check all related verses and draw our conclusions from all of these together. When this is done, it becomes apparent that there are numerous examples of actual named people who were *righteous*. Please note the following Scriptures:

This is the account of Noah. **Noah was a righteous man**, blameless among the people of his time, and he walked with God. (Gen 6:9)

Because **Joseph her husband was a righteous man** and did not want to expose her to public disgrace, he had in mind to divorce her quietly. (Mat 1:19)

Now there was a man in Jerusalem called **Simeon, who was righteous** and devout. He was waiting for the consolation of Israel, and the Holy Spirit was upon him. (Luke 2:25)

And so upon you will come all the righteous blood that has been shed on earth, from the blood of **righteous Abel to the blood of Zechariah** son of Berekiah, whom you murdered between the temple and the altar. (Mat 23:35)

and if he rescued **Lot, a righteous man**, who was distressed by the filthy lives of lawless men (for that righteous man, living among them day after day, was tormented in his righteous soul by the lawless deeds he saw and heard) (2 Pet 2:7,8)

Was not our ancestor **Abraham considered righteous** for what he did when he offered his son Isaac on the altar? (James 2:21)

According to these Scriptures, Noah, Joseph, Simeon, Abel, Zechariah, Lot and Abraham are all clearly cited as being *righteous*. If we had no other Scriptures except any one of these we should know **something is terribly wrong with the eternal security idea that there are none that are righteous and that we are all sinners, even Christians**. (Since we have a whole chapter in this book devoted to the false concept that we are all sinners, including Christians, it will not be dealt with here.)

Besides the above list, there is also another important Scripture:

> You are witnesses, and so is God, of how holy, **righteous** and blame-less we were among you who believed. (1 Th 2:10)

The pronoun *we* refers to Paul and his companions (Silas and Timothy). They too are specific examples of *righteous* people by name. So now we have Noah, Joseph, Simeon, Abel, Zechariah, Lot, Abraham, Paul, Silas and Timothy.

The Unnamed Righteous

Besides the actual people that are labeled *righteous*, there are scores of other Scriptures which refer to the unnamed *righteous*. Please ponder just some of these many Scriptures. The following list is only from the New Testament:

> that you may be sons of your Father in heaven. He causes his sun to rise on the evil and the good, and sends rain on **the righteous and the unrighteous**. (Mat 5:45)

> But go and learn what this means: "I desire mercy, not sacrifice." For I have not come to call the **righteous**, but **sinners**. (Mat 9:13)

> Anyone who receives a prophet because he is a prophet will receive a prophet's reward, and anyone who receives **a righteous man** be-cause he is **a righteous man** will receive **a righteous man's reward**. (Mat 10:41)

> For I tell you the truth, many prophets and **righteous men** longed to see what you see but did not see it, and to hear what you hear but did not hear it. (Mat 13:17)

> Then **the righteous** will shine like the sun in the kingdom of their Father. He who has ears, let him hear. (Mat 13:43)

> This is how it will be at the end of the age. The angels will come and separate **the wicked** from **the righteous** (Mat 13:49)

Woe to you, teachers of the law and Pharisees, you hypocrites! You build tombs for the prophets and decorate **the graves of the righteous**. (Mat 23:29)

Then **the righteous will answer him**, "Lord, when did we see you hungry and feed you, or thirsty and give you something to drink?" (Mat 25:37)

Then they will go away to eternal punishment, but **the righteous to eternal life**. (Mat 25:46)

On hearing this, Jesus said to them, "It is not the healthy who need a doctor, but the sick. I have not come to call **the righteous, but sinners**." (Mark 2:17)

And he will go on before the Lord, in the spirit and power of Elijah, to turn the hearts of the fathers to their children and the disobedient to **the wisdom of the righteous**—to make ready a people prepared for the Lord. (Luke 1:17)

I have not come to call **the righteous, but sinners to repentance**. (Luke 5:32)

and you will be blessed. Although they cannot repay you, you will be repaid at **the resurrection of the righteous**. (Luke 14:14)

I tell you that in the same way there will be more rejoicing in heaven over one sinner who repents than over **ninety-nine righteous persons who do not need to repent**. (Luke 15:7)

and I have the same hope in God as these men, that there will be a resurrection of both **the righteous** and **the wicked**. (Acts 24:15)

For in the gospel a righteousness from God is revealed, a righteousness that is by faith from first to last, just as it is written: **"The righteous will live by faith**." (Rom 1:17)

For it is not those who hear the law who are righteous in God's sight, but it is those who obey the law who will be **declared righteous**. (Rom 2:13)

Therefore no one will be **declared righteous** in his sight by observing the law; rather, through the law we become conscious of sin. (Rom 3:20)

Very rarely will anyone **die for a righteous man**, though for a good man someone might possibly dare to die. (Rom 5:7)

For just as through the disobedience of the one man the many were made sinners, so also through the obedience of the one man the many will be **made righteous**. (Rom 5:19)

Clearly no one is justified before God by the law, because, **"The righteous will live by faith."** (Gal 3:11)

We also know that law is made **not for the righteous** but for lawbreakers and rebels, the ungodly and sinful, the unholy and irreligious; for those who kill their fathers or mothers, for murderers, (1 Tim 1:9)

to the church of the firstborn, whose names are written in heaven. You have come to God, the judge of all men, to **the spirits of righteous men** made perfect (Heb 12:23)

Therefore confess your sins to each other and pray for each other so that you may be healed. **The prayer of a righteous man** is powerful and effective. (James 5:16)

For the eyes of the Lord are on **the righteous and his ears are attentive to their prayer**, but the face of the Lord is against those who do evil. (1 Pet 3:12)

And, "If it is hard for **the righteous** to be saved, what will become of the ungodly and the sinner?" (1 Pet 4:18)

Dear children, do not let anyone lead you astray. **He who does what is right is righteous, just as he is righteous**. (1 John 3:7)

Remember This

To say that there are none who are *righteous* is the same as saying that **all are *unrighteous*.** If that was true, then every person, with no exception, will **not inherit the kingdom of God**:

Know ye not that **the unrighteous shall not inherit the kingdom of God?** Be not deceived: neither fornicators, nor idolaters, nor adulterers, nor effeminate, nor abusers of themselves with mankind, Nor thieves, nor covetous, nor drunkards, nor revilers, nor extortioners, shall inherit the kingdom of God. (1 Cor 6:9,10, KJV)

To not inherit the Kingdom of God is to be thrown into the lake of fire.

The Meaning of Roman 3:10

The meaning of Romans 3:10 is that **all people without salvation are unrighteous**, that is, not even one is *righteous*. This pertains to both Jew and Gentile alike as Paul was stressing in that chapter. Please note some other details about those that are not *righteous* from the context:

What shall we conclude then? Are we any better? Not at all! We have already made the charge that Jews and Gentiles alike are all under sin. As it is written: **There is no one righteous, not even one**; there is no one who understands, no one who seeks God. All have turned away, they have together become worthless; there is no one who does good, not even one. Their throats are open graves; their tongues practice deceit. The poison of vipers is on their lips. Their mouths are full of cursing and bitterness. Their feet are swift to shed blood; ruin and misery mark their ways, and the way of peace they do not know. There is no fear of God before their eyes. (Rom 3:9-18)

The people that are **not righteous** are also mentioned with the following:

- no one who understands
- no one who seeks God
- they have together become worthless
- there is no one who does good, not even one
- there is no fear of God before their eyes

Paul was referring to the following Scriptures when he gave us Romans 3:9-18:

The fool says in his heart, "There is no God." They are corrupt, their deeds are vile; there is no one who does good. The LORD looks down from heaven on the sons of men to see if there are any who understand, any who seek God. All have turned aside, they have together become corrupt; there is no one who does good, not even one. (Psa 14:1-3)

An oracle is within my heart concerning **the sinfulness of the wicked**: There is no fear of God before his eyes. For in his own eyes he flatters himself too much to detect or hate his sin. The words of his mouth are wicked and deceitful; he has ceased to be wise and to do good. (Psa 36:1-3)

In other words, Paul was not referring to the follower of Christ, but all *wicked* people if they are Jew or Gentile, even the *fool*, who doesn't even think there is a God.

The Righteous

One becomes *righteous* at the point of a trusting-submitting faith in Jesus, which includes repentance. Basic characteristics of the *righteous* include the following:

(1)   they don't have anything to repent of (Lk. 15:7);
(2)   they are not doing evil (1 Peter 3:12);
(3)   they do what is right (1 John 3:7).

It is also clear from multiple Scriptures that the righteous will live because of his *faith*:

See, he is puffed up; his desires are not upright—but **the righteous will live by his faith** (Hab 2:4)

For in the gospel a righteousness from God is revealed, a righteousness that is by faith from first to last, just as it is written: "**The righteous will live by faith.**" (Rom 1:17)

Clearly no one is justified before God by the law, because, "**The righteous will live by faith.**" (Gal 3:11)

But **my righteous one will live by faith**. And if he shrinks back, I will not be pleased with him. (Heb 10:38)

If one is not *righteous*, then he is in the only other group possible. Sometimes that group is referred to as wicked, unrighteous, ungodly, unholy, sinners, evil, unsaved or the like. In other words, if one is not *righteous* he is on the road to hell at this very moment and is in a desperate need to repent. **We must never forget that only the *righteous* will go to *eternal life*:**

Then they will go away to eternal punishment, but the **righteous to eternal life**. (Mat 25:46)

You Can Become Righteous

Again, one must repent (turn from his sins) or he will perish. Hence, the faith in Jesus that is needed to be considered righteous is a trusting and submitting faith—one that obeys. Furthermore, **it is imperative to endure to the very end of your life to enter God's paradise kingdom** (Mt. 10:22; Heb. 3:14 and Rev. 2:10,11). If you are a real Christian now, you are *righteous*, **but sin can change that righteous standing and bring you to your spiritual death, just like it did for both Adam and Eve**. Because of this truth, Paul told Timothy (who was righteous) *to keep himself pure* (1 Tim. 5:22). This is under the umbrella of the *grace* that Paul preached and by which we are saved. We read this multiple times in Ezekiel:

Again, when a righteous man turns from his righteousness and does evil, and I put a stumbling block before him, **he will die**. Since you did not warn him, **he will die for his sin**. The righteous things he did will not be remembered, and I will hold you accountable for his blood. But if you do warn the righteous man not to sin and he does not sin, he will surely live because he took warning, and you will have saved yourself. (Ezek 3:20, 21)

But if a righteous man turns from his righteousness and commits sin and does the same detestable things the wicked man does, will he live? None of the righteous things he has done will be remembered. Because of the unfaithfulness he is guilty of and because of the sins he has committed, **he will die.** (Ezek 18:24)

If a righteous man turns from his righteousness and commits sin, **he will die for it**; because of the sin he has committed **he will die.** (Ezek 18:26)

If I tell the righteous man that he will surely live, but then he trusts in his righteousness and does evil, none of the righteous things he has done will be remembered; **he will die for the evil he has done.** (Ezek 33:13)

If a righteous man turns from his righteousness and does evil, **he will die for it.** (Ezek 33:18)

35

Apostasy Occurs
Among Christians

Apostasy (departure from the faith) is a definite possibility among Christians, even though it is sometimes vehemently denied by the security-in-sin teachers, better known as *eternal security* or *the perseverance of the saints* teachers. In fact, apostasy is taught so often throughout the New Testament that it is difficult to believe that anyone sincerely desiring truth could miss it. To be precise **it is found in almost every New Testament book. The only two exceptions are Philemon and 3 John.** Sometimes it is clearly shown as much as six or more times in a single book, such as in Hebrews or 1 Timothy. In other books, departure (or its possibility) from the Christian faith is shown four or five times. **Hence, there is sufficient evidence in the Scriptures to know with absolute certainty that apostasy can and does occur. Therefore it is a real, deadly danger among the saved in our hour. To be aware of this fact will help keep a Christian on his spiritual guard for survival's sake (John 15:18-16:1). Knowledge of this is a preventative. On the other hand, to deny this glaring truth and think you must always *stand firm* is to set yourself and your listeners up for a spiritual *fall*.** True grace teaching is emphatic on this:

> So, if you think you are standing firm, **be careful that you don't fall!** (1 Cor. 10:12)

(This is reason enough to leave any so-called church that teaches eternal security and take as many out of there with you that you can.)

Below are specific verses showing the possibility of apostasy, or actual examples of such, in 25 of the 27 New Testament books—that is **a total of 93% of the New Testament books which cite specific examples or imply the possibility that true Christians can go back to wickedness (and lose their salvation).**

Matthew

At that time **many will turn away from the faith** and will betray and hate each other, and many false prophets will appear and deceive many people (24:10,11).

Mark

"You will all fall away," Jesus told them, "for it is written: I will strike the shepherd, and the **sheep** will be scattered ...." (14:27).

NOTE: Jesus taught it is the *sheep*, **not those** *never saved*, **who fall away.**

Luke

"... **They believe for a while**, but in the time of testing they **fall away**" (8:13).

John

From this time many of **his disciples turned back and no longer followed him** (6:66).

Acts

"... **there will be a resurrection of both the righteous and the wicked. So I strive always to keep my conscience clear** before God and man" (24:15,16).

Romans

You will say then, "Branches were broken off so that I could be grafted in." Granted. But they were broken off because of unbelief, and **you stand by faith. Do not be arrogant, but be afraid**. For if God did not spare the natural branches, **he will not spare you either**. Consider therefore the kindness and sternness of God: sternness **to those who fell**, but kindness to you, provided that you continue in his kindness. **Otherwise, you also will be cut off.** And if they do not persist in unbelief, they will be grafted in, for God is able to graft them in again (11:19-23).

1 Corinthians

But I discipline my body and make it my slave, **so that, after I have preached to others, I myself will not be disqualified** (9:27, NASB).

2 Corinthians

Examine yourselves to see whether you are in the faith; test yourselves. Do you not realize that Christ Jesus is in you—unless, of course, you fail the test? (13:5).

Galatians

I am astonished that you are so **quickly deserting the one who called you by the grace of Christ and are turning to a different gospel**—which is really no gospel at all. Evidently some people are throwing you into confusion and are trying to pervert the gospel of Christ (1:6,7).

Ephesians

For of this you can be sure: No immoral, impure or greedy person—such a man is an idolater—has any inheritance in the kingdom of Christ and of God. Let no one deceive you with empty words, for because of such things God's wrath comes on those who are disobedient. Therefore do not be partners with them (5:5-7).

Philippians

I want to know Christ and the power of his resurrection and the fellowship of sharing in his sufferings, becoming like him in his death, and so, **somehow, to attain to the resurrection from the dead. Not that I have already obtained all this, or have already been made perfect,** but I press on to take hold of that for which Christ Jesus took hold of me (3:10-12).

Colossians

But now he has reconciled you by Christ's physical body through death to present you holy in his sight, without blemish and free from accusation—**if you continue in your faith,** established and firm, not moved from the hope held out in the gospel. This is the gospel that you heard and that has been proclaimed to every creature under heaven, and of which I, Paul, have become a servant (1:22,23).

1 Thessalonians

It is God's will that you should be sanctified: that you should avoid sexual immorality; that each of you should learn to control his own body in a way that is holy and honorable, not in passionate lust like the heathen, who do not know God; and that in this matter no one should wrong his brother or take advantage of him. The Lord will punish men for all such sins, as we have already told you and warned you. **For God did not call us to be impure, but to live a holy life. Therefore, he who rejects this instruction does not reject man but God, who gives you his Holy Spirit** (4:3-8).

2 Thessalonians

Let no one in any way deceive you, for it will not come **unless the apostasy comes first,** and the man of lawlessness is revealed, the son of destruction (2:3, NASB).

1 Timothy

Holding on to faith and a good conscience. **Some have rejected these and so have shipwrecked their faith**. Among them are Hymenaeus and Alexander, whom I have handed over to Satan to be taught not to blaspheme (1:19,20).

2 Timothy

Avoid godless chatter, because those who indulge in it will become more and more ungodly. Their teaching will spread like gangrene. **Among them are Hymenaeus and Philetus, who have wandered away from the truth. They say that the resurrection has already taken place, and they destroy the faith of some** (2:16-18).

Titus

So that, having been justified by his grace, **we might become heirs having the hope of eternal life** (3:7).

Hebrews

For in the case of those who have once been enlightened and have tasted of the heavenly gift and have been made partakers of the Holy Spirit, and have tasted the good word of God and the powers of the age to come, and *then* **have fallen away, it is impossible to renew them again to repentance**, since they again crucify to themselves the Son of God and put Him to open shame (6:4-6, NASB).

James

My brethren, if any among you strays from the truth, and one turns him back, let him know that he who turns a sinner from the error of his way will **save his soul from death**, and will cover a multitude of sins (5:19,20, NASB).

1 Peter

As obedient children, **do not conform to the evil desires you had when you lived in ignorance**. (1 Pet 1:14)

2 Peter

If they have **escaped the corruption of the world by knowing our Lord and Savior Jesus Christ and are again entangled in it and overcome, they are worse off at the end than they were at the beginning**. It would have been better for them not to have known the way of righteousness, than to have known it and then to **turn their backs on the sacred command that was passed on to them**. Of them the proverbs are true: "**A dog returns to its vomit**," and, "**A sow that is washed goes back to her wallowing in the mud**" (2:20-22).

1 John

See that what you have heard from the beginning remains in you. **If it does, you also will remain in the Son and in the Father. And this is what he promised us—even eternal life** (2:24,25).

2 John

Anyone who runs ahead and does not continue in the teaching of Christ **does not have God**; whoever **continues** in the teaching **has both the Father and the Son** (1:9).

Jude

Though you already know all this, I want to remind you that **the Lord delivered his people out of Egypt, but later destroyed those who did not believe. And the angels who did not keep their positions of authority but abandoned their own home—these he has kept in darkness, bound with everlasting chains for judgment on the great Day** (1:5,6).

Revelation

> Do not be afraid of what you are about to suffer. I tell you, the devil will put some of you in prison to test you, and you will suffer persecution for ten days. **Be faithful, even to the point of death, and I will give you the crown of life**. He who has an ear, let him hear what the Spirit says to the churches. **He who overcomes will not be hurt at all by the second death** (2:10,11).

NOTE: The second death is another name for *the lake of fire* (Rev. 21:8).

The Present Massive Deception

With all of the above Scriptural evidence, which contradicts the security-in-sin gospel (eternal security), one has to wonder how Bible-believers can remain in such denial about this reality. Apparently, the slick-talking, ear-tickling eternal security teachers, with their infernal talents of distorting the Word of God, have been so successful with their lies that **multitudes of souls remain in jeopardy**. Dear reader, **what are you going to do about this urgent need to get this vital truth out, before it is too late?**

36

10 Common Misconceptions About A Conditional Security

The following are misconceptions and strawman arguments that eternal security people use to falsely accuse and discredit Christians like us who teach a conditional security for the believer. Certainly, sometimes the eternal security teachers will intentionally imply any, some or all of the following to dishonor our beliefs when they are teaching. Here is what they slanderously say about us:

- Such people don't believe in grace.
- Such people don't believe in the blood of Jesus.
- Such people don't believe in the infinite work of Christ.
- Such people don't believe in the free gift of eternal life.
- Such people believe in a works salvation.
- Such people are in legalism.
- Such people believe in sinless perfection.
- Such people are trying to save themselves.
- Such people are unsaved.
- Such people think they lose their salvation every time they sin.

Setting The Record Straight

Let's review that list again but this time supply Biblical answers/comments to clear away these misconceptions about Christians who embrace a conditional security:

■   Such people don't believe in *grace*.

We believe and know without a doubt that we are saved by grace, as the Bible declares (Acts 15:11; Eph. 2:5, 8, etc.). But after we do get saved we also know we can *fall from grace* (Gal. 5:2-4). If such occurs, then Christ has become of *no effect* unto such people, according to Scripture (Gal. 5:4). We also know there are other ways in which we can lose our salvation, according to Scripture.

■   Such people don't believe in *the blood of Jesus*.

We believe it is only by the blood of Jesus that we can be purged from our sins (Heb. 1:3) and set free from its slavery (Rev. 1:5). We contact Jesus' precious, saving blood at the point of a trusting-submitting faith in the Lord Jesus when we turn from all sins and get born again. But we also know some have *treated as an unholy thing the blood of the covenant that sanctified them* (Heb. 10:29) and have since become enemies of God with **raging fire awaiting them** (Heb. 10:27). See also James 4:4.

■   Such people don't believe in the *infinite work of Christ*.

We know our redemption was paid for in full at the cross by Christ alone when he said, *It is finished* (John 19:30). But we also know the Lord Jesus and his apostles taught those already saved that they would have to **endure and remain faithful to God to the end to be saved and not be hurt by the second death** (Mt. 10:22; Rev. 2:10,11; Heb. 3:14).

■   Such people don't believe in the *free gift* of eternal life.

We believe that eternal life is a *gift*, as Rom. 6:23 declares. But we also believe the previous verse which describes a real Christian, and what leads to *holiness* resulting with *eternal life*:

But now that you have been set free from sin and have become slaves to God, the benefit you reap leads to holiness, and the result is eternal life. For the wages of sin is death, but the gift of God is eternal life in Christ Jesus our Lord (Rom. 6:22,23).

Eternal life is gift, but it is also a hope, yet to be reaped in the age to come, for the ones who persist in doing good and don't give up sowing to please the Spirit of God (Titus 3:7; Mark 10:30; Rom. 2:7; Gal. 6:8,9; etc.).

■ Such people believe in a *works salvation.*

As already stated we believe we are saved by *grace.* But we also believe *grace* is best described in the following passage:

It teaches us to say "No" to ungodliness and worldly passions, and to live self-controlled, upright and godly lives in this present age (Titus 2:12).

Paul also believed and wrote about salvation (by grace) and gave the following to those who had already been saved:

The one who sows to please his sinful nature, from that nature **will reap destruction**; the one who sows to please the Spirit, from the Spirit **will reap eternal life**. Let us not become weary in doing good, for at the proper time we will reap a harvest **if we do not give up.** Therefore, as we have opportunity, let us do good to all people, especially to those who belong to the family of believers (Gal. 6:8-10).

■ Such people are in *legalism.*

Paul taught against *legalism,* yet taught the aforementioned facts about salvation, which the eternal security teachers cannot reconcile with their security-in-sin "gospel." In other words, those Scriptures, and others like them, are under the umbrella of *grace,* not *legalism.*

■ Such people believe in *sinless perfection.*

We do not believe in sinless perfection, as some have in the past. All sins are not the same in their effect on our souls. Some sins are greater than others (Jn. 19:11). One type is eternal (Mk. 3:29), while others are not. Another type of sin is uniquely against our bodies, while other sins are outside our bodies (1 Cor. 6:18). 1 Jn. 5:16 declares there is a sin that does not lead to death while there is a sin that leads to death. Sins such as worry

(Phil. 4:6), unthankfulness (Col. 2:7, 3:15; Lk. 17:11-18) and not being completely humble and gentle (Eph. 4:2) are not included in any of the lists of sins that will send people to the lake of fire, even if they were once saved. However, other sins certainly will send any person to hell if they die unrepentant, even a person who was once saved. (See 1 Cor. 6:9,10; Rev. 21:8; Gal. 5:19-21; Eph. 5:5,6; Jude 7; Rev. 22:15; etc.).

■   Such people are trying to *save themselves*.

We are not trying to save ourselves. Jesus is the only Savior (Acts 4:12) and our eyes are on him for our salvation. **All 100% of our trust is in Jesus alone for salvation and not our good deeds too, even though we have good deeds**. We are his sheep, and have salvation, as long as we continue to follow him (John 10:27). Because our faith is alive we have good deeds (James 2:17).

■   Such people are *unsaved*.

We are not unsaved because we reject eternal security. **Such an untruth cannot be tied to any Scripture**. We do acknowledge that Christian people can become unsaved, though, by believing/preaching a false gospel, committing certain types of sin or disowning Jesus during persecution (1 Cor. 15:2; 1 John 2:24,25; Gal. 1:8,9; Rev. 21:8; Eph. 5:5-7; Gal. 5:19-21; Mt. 10:33; etc.).

■   Such people think they lose their salvation *every time they sin*.

We do not believe we lose our salvation every time we sin. There are many sins that will not damn any Christian to eternal fire if committed, such as: worry, not being completely humble and gentle and not overflowing with thanksgiving. Never are such sins included in any Biblical list which states who will *not inherit the kingdom of God* and/or be thrown into the *lake of fire* such as the sexually immoral, drunkards, idolaters, murderers, liars, etc. (1 Cor. 6:9,10; Eph. 5:5-7; Rev. 21:8).

We get all 100% of our beliefs from the Bible and sincerely have studied it for decades with a willingness to change accordingly. Our beliefs are backed up with appropriate Scripture used in its proper context as well as other supporting Scriptures. **We have found the eternal security pro-**

ponents to be the ones who don't understand the Bible and will misrepresent our beliefs to make their own seem more credible, as just shown.

37

Eternal Security Teachers Are Very Dangerous People

Eternal security teachers are very *dangerous* people. Don't ever forget this fact and warning. Though it may seem like an exaggeration, they are *vastly more dangerous* than *quack medical doctors* or even *serial murderers*. This is because they can adversely affect you throughout all *eternity* and not just shorten your physical life. It will be your *eternal soul*—your most valuable possession—that will suffer by the deception they put you in.

Their False Salvation Plan

The eternal security teachers want you to believe the *exact opposite* to the Bible in areas related to *salvation* that can, and will almost always, adversely affect you from entering the kingdom of God. See 1 Cor. 10:12 and Rom. 11:20-22. Their message is not only in error, but is a definite denial of God's truth. One such example is their contradiction of Jesus' teaching to his apostles—"But whoever disowns me before men, I will disown him before my Father in heaven" (Mt. 10:33). They openly teach that you can disown Jesus but he won't disown you! Another example is their idea of *bondage* being walking in holiness and the fear of God. Scripture says that keeping God's commands is *not burdensome* (1 John 5:3) and that Jesus' yoke is easy and his burden is light (Mt. 11:30). Eternal security is not the *Christian* message, but a dangerous counterfeit and distortion, though it uses Biblical terms.

The bottom line in their security message is to convince the Christian that he can drift to the extreme of being an adulterer and murderer like King David, an idolater like Solomon, disown Jesus like Peter and live worse than the pagans as the unnamed man of 1 Cor. 5 did, and remain saved while unrepentant. Be assured they won't openly admit this with the aforementioned clarity, but this will become evident in their teachings as they mishandle the Scriptures and allow for every sort of evil in their goal to convince you that there is *salvation* security in sin. All eternal security teachers, with no exception, believe such about David, etc. and want you to receive this deadly spiritual poison too. They will make this a priority as they avoid hundreds of clear Scriptures that dismantle their thesis and twist dozens of others to allow for wickedness, blasphemy, continued lukewarmness and doctrinal apostasy for the Christian. To them this is *grace* as well as the *gospel*.

Poison Not Food

Instead of getting wholesome spiritual food for your soul about salvation from them, you will get deadly spiritual poison. This poison will come as they contradict the biblical message regarding the deadly dangers of sin in the life of a Christian, the need to live holy for salvation, the vital necessity to endure to the end, etc. **The so-called *truth* they spread and defend will lead those so deceived into the flames of hell, while they think they are on the road to heaven in their sins at the expense of their *rewards*.**

Again, don't forget that their unconditional security-in-sin message is part of their *salvation* message, but it is not the one and only salvation message of the Bible. It flatly rejects and opposes the conditions of the true gospel of grace (1 Cor. 15:2; Col. 1:23). It is a false gospel (Gal. 1:8,9) and a bogus grace message that is a license for immorality (Jude 3,4). Please see the definite differences between their spurious salvation/gospel message and the Christian one as shown in another one of our chapters on pages 50-52.

Don't Support a False Gospel

Since the eternal security teachers are doing such lethal harm to so many souls, how can any Christian rightly justify helping, supporting or even verbally encouraging the spread of their *false salvation* and security-in-sin message? The truth is: Christians must be careful not to share in their *wicked work* by helping them or by providing a platform for their poisonous message to go forth. See 2 John 10,11. To aid and abet the spread of their deadly message is serious. Surely there are multitudes in hell at this moment because they were deceived by these harmless looking eternal security teachers and the so-called *freedoms* they learned from them under their perverted version of *grace*.

It is a fact that our *behavior* is affected by what we accept as *truth*. If you accept as truth that you are, without doubt, going to enter heaven after you die because you are eternally secure, you will act accordingly by: (1) Lowering your guard that you must be on to remain faithful to the very end to enter God's paradise kingdom (Rev. 2:10,11; Mt. 10:22; Heb. 3:14). (2) You will not make a continuous and agonizing effort to enter the kingdom doors as Jesus commanded (Lk. 13:23,24), since you have been deceived into thinking this is legalism and a work's salvation. (3) You will not keep yourself from sin (1 Tim. 5:22; 1 John 5:21; etc.), since you have been deceived into thinking that God is keeping you and you better not be trying to keep yourself. The same goes for *holding on*, even though Jesus taught Christians this very truth (Rev. 2:25; 3:11) and it is a foundational part of the real gospel of grace (1 Cor. 15:2).

The Victims

Furthermore, the *victims* of eternal security teaching who lose their salvation will never be aware of it and therefore, will never repent of their sins for salvation's sake, especially if they think their future sins have been forgiven before they were ever committed. We have often seen that it is only after eternal security proponents realize this doctrine is false that they repent of their sins. (They remain unrepentant while in this belief.) This is more proof that the doctrine of eternal security is a deadly snare and a lethal trap for all so deceived and all God fearing Christians, with no exception, should strenuously battle against it.

The Christian walk, in part, is a fight over God's truth. Since the eternal security teachers are countering God's truth, they are *enemies* of the true gospel of grace. They must be fought against and refuted. **This is war!** The battle can be fierce, but we have been called to be soldiers of Christ who are to endure hardship (2 Tim. 2:3). Since they have big money powers, publishers, radio stations, etc. behind them and we that embrace the truth are in the minority, we have our work cut out for us. **But dear Christian never forget we have God and His truth on our side!**

Count The Cost

Many will think you are *a heretic* and teaching *a works salvation* because you oppose the big named respected eternal security teachers and stand on Scripture and Scripture alone. We have seen this numerous times. **That doesn't change the fact that these dangerous-but-innocent-looking popular teachers should not just be ignored but strongly opposed, even at the expense of your doctrinal reputation. And remember this: Just because they are doctrinally sound in some areas doesn't mean their so-called** *gospel* **is not dangerous. Neither should we view them in a favorable way. Be on your guard against their other teachings as well because the eternal security heresy will permeate various things they proclaim.**

If God has opened your spiritual eyes to the lethal dangers of eternal security teaching you will be held accountable for this precious knowledge. Therefore, oppose this teaching with the same intensity you would some known false prophet also proclaiming a counterfeit gospel. As Christians we have been called to do this type of battle. For the sake of truth and all those who can yet be helped, *fight the good fight of the faith* **(1 Tim. 6:12). Precious souls hang in the balance. We are battling for eternity. Remember that the eternal security teachers are** *vastly more dangerous than quack medical doctors or even serial murderers.*

Finally, to have your family and especially your children subjected to their teaching will produce an *unholy* and *disobedient offspring*. We have received emails that can testify to this very thing.

38

Is Believing On Jesus The Same as Obeying Him?

Because of various doctrines of demons, many think they can believe on Jesus without obeying him. This, however, is not the message of the Bible, but a dangerous misunderstanding and spiritual snare. Please note the following passage cited from two different reputable translations:

> Whoever **believes in the Son** has eternal life; whoever **disobeys the Son** will not see life, but must endure God's wrath (John 3:36, NRSV).

> He who **believes in the Son** has eternal life; but he who **does not obey the Son** shall not see life, but the wrath of God abides on him (John 3:36, NASB).

The King James Version renders this same verse as:

> He that believeth on the Son hath everlasting life: and he that believeth not the Son shall not see life; but the wrath of God abideth on him.

The Greek word translated as *believeth not* in that verse is *apeitheo* and it means: *not believe, disobedient, obey not, unbelieving*. This alone makes the crucial point loud and clear about *disobedience being a manifestation of unbelief.*

Remember also that there are only two types of people which are sometimes referred to as the *saved* or the *unsaved*, the *sheep* or the *goats*, etc. But in the above passage, these two types of people are either mentioned as **those that believe on the Son** or those **that disobey the Son**. In other words, again it becomes apparent that *unbelief* in Jesus is synonymous with *disobedience* to him, while *believing in Jesus* equals *obeying him*. That is a vital truth we all need to remember because it helps us understand the Biblical meaning of the only kind of belief in Jesus that brings salvation. But the same truth is also shown in the following passage:

> And to whom did He swear that they should not enter His rest, but to those who were **disobedient**? And so we see that they were not able to enter because of **unbelief** (Heb. 3:18,19, NASB).

Notice again how *disobedience* is equated to *unbelief.* Hence, we see again the meaning of unbelief and an important insight about disobedience. In other words, *disobedience* **is a manifestation of** *unbelief.* **Can it then be stated that many who at one time truly believed on Jesus are now in unbelief as is made evident by their disobedience? The answer is a resounding yes.** Jesus taught:

> They **believe for a while**, but in the time of testing they fall away (Luke 8:13).

Jesus taught a true believer could turn into an unbeliever and consequently die spiritually. This is especially important in a day when so many have been deceived by the security in sin gospel commonly called *eternal security* or *the perseverance of the saints*. In other words, a true Christian can afterwards lose his salvation, as has happened numerous times, according to the Bible. To enter God's paradise kingdom after death, a person who was previously *born again* must endure persecution and hatred for being a Christian, bring forth good fruit and (among other things) continue to believe on Jesus, which will manifest in simple *obedience*.

Besides all of the above, remember the following relevant Scriptures:

> He [Jesus] became the source of eternal salvation **for all who obey him** (Heb 5:9).

> Those **who have done good** will rise to live, and those **who have done evil** will rise to be condemned (John 5:29) .

Scripture Index

Other Books By Dan Corner

The Believer's Conditional Security

Exhaustive (801 pages) ■ Contemporary ■ Comprehensive (195+ sources)
Fully documented (700+ footnotes) ■ Fully indexed
Historical, little-known facts

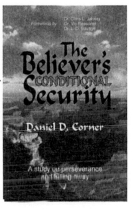

The Believer's Conditional Security is the most exhaustive and comprehensive refutation to the once saved, always saved (OSAS) teaching ever written. It deals a deathblow to OSAS through a close examination of the Scriptures, exposes the real John Calvin and unmasks the Synod of Dort. Stanley, Swindoll, MacArthur, Hunt, Hanegraaff, Ankerberg and many others are quoted and refuted.

Softback or CD $19.50
Hardback $29.50
Call (724) 632-3210 for bulk discounts

$17.00 E-book
(E-book and CD are for PC only and require IE 4.0 or higher, obtainable free from www.microsoft.com)

The Gospel According to Charles Stanley
This shocking and devastating exposé should be read by every professing Christian. (42 page booklet)
$2.50 (Softback—Specify English or Spanish)
$2.50 Voice Book

$1.50 E-book
(E-book and CD are for PC only and require IE 4.0 or higher, obtainable free from www.microsoft.com) **Call (724) 632-3210 for bulk discounts.**

Is This The Mary Of The Bible?
Comparing Catholicism's Mary to the Biblical Mary (249 page book)
$11.50 (Softback)

Unmasking John MacArthur's Calvinistic Version Of Saving Faith

This book reveals some of the inconsistent and unscriptural declarations of MacArthur's *holiness* teachings. (52 page booklet)
$5.95 (Softback)

A Critique Of Gail Riplinger's Scholarship and KJV Onlyism

Loaded with shocking information. (54 page booklet)
$5.95 (Softback)

A Study On Biblical Salvation

This book will help to clear up the confusion that exists regarding the true way to enter the Kingdom. (54 page booklet)
$5.95 (Softback)

Audio-Visual Dramatized Gospel CD

Stirring, dramatized 23 minute presentation with multiple voices, beautiful music and sound effects. Includes transcript and original artwork.
$3.50 (PC only)

The Dramatized Gospel CD

Stirring, dramatized 23 minute gospel presentation with multiple voices, beautiful music and sound effects. VERY POWERFUL!
$2.50 (Not Mac compatible)

Postage charges IN USA
Up to $20.00: add $3.50 | $20.01–50.00: add $5.00
$50.01–100.00: add 10% of total | $100.01 and Up: add 8% of total
Postage charges OUTSIDE USA
Up to $20.00: add $10.00 | $20.01–35.00: add $18.00
$35.01–50.00: add $22.00 | $50.01–$100.00: add $10.00 plus 35%
Over $100.00: add $10.00 plus 24%

Evangelical Outreach
PO Box 265, Washington, PA 15301
(724) 632-3210 ■ www.evangelicaloutreach.org
contender@evangelicaloutreach.org